RESERVOIRS
of STRENGTH

RESERVOIRS
of STRENGTH
Lessons from the Book of James

Gerald M. Bilkes

Reformation Heritage Books
Grand Rapids, Michigan

Reservoirs of Strength
© 2017 by Gerald M. Bilkes

Reformation Heritage Books
2965 Leonard St. NE
Grand Rapids, MI 49525
616-977-0889 / Fax 616-285-3246
orders@heritagebooks.org
www.heritagebooks.org

Printed in the United States of America
17 18 19 20 21 22/10 9 8 7 6 5 4 3 2 1

Library of Congress Cataloging-in-Publication Data

Names: Bilkes, Gerald M., author.
Title: Reservoirs of strength : lessons from the Book of James / Gerald M. Bilkes.
Description: Grand Rapids, Michigan : Reformation Heritage Books, 2017.
Identifiers: LCCN 2017050950 (print) | LCCN 2017052373 (ebook) | ISBN 9781601785756 (epub) | ISBN 9781601785749 (pbk. : alk. paper)
Subjects: LCSH: Bible. James—Commentaries.
Classification: LCC BS2785.53 (ebook) | LCC BS2785.53 .B55 2017 (print) | DDC 227/.9107—dc23
LC record available at https://lccn.loc.gov/2017050950

For additional Reformed literature, request a free book list from Reformation Heritage Books at the above regular or e-mail address.

Contents

INTRODUCING JAMES,
A SHEPHERD OF SOULS

James 1

All believers endure trials and tribulation. The early Christians did, and today we must as well. Christ did not hide this truth from His followers but prepared them for it: "In the world ye shall have tribulation" (John 16:33). A generation later, Paul taught that "we must through much tribulation enter into the kingdom of God" (Acts 14:22). The exact makeup of trials in your life might be yours and no one else's, but all Christians pass through the fire of refining that is called tribulation.

If you are a Christian, what is your tribulation? And what is it doing for you? Or, what are you making out of the trouble you endure? Do you have somewhere to go in your trials? Do you feel like you are coming apart at the seams? Are you between battles and trying to catch your breath? Can you say with Paul, "I am exceeding joyful in all [my] tribulation" (2 Cor. 7:4)?

Paul wasn't the only one who was joyful in tribulation. James opens up a brief letter to very early and mostly new Christians with a bold challenge: "Count it all joy when ye fall into divers temptations" (1:2). Do you want to know how to do that? James will show us. As a pastor, a shepherd of souls, he knows the way to the quiet streams that can strengthen us in trials. In this little book, he has left us an inspired map leading us to reservoirs of strength in times of testing.

Backcountry of the World

The days of the apostles were remarkable, with many unprecedented things taking place as the early church grew through unlikely means. Common people, such as fishermen, from "backcountry" areas of the world, like Galilee, turned things upside down as they preached the gospel boldly, beginning at Jerusalem and throughout the world. They took this gospel to synagogues, to marketplaces, to governors' palaces, and to prisons. Everywhere it went, this gospel showed its power. Strongholds of darkness and idolatry were torn down. People's lives were transformed. Communities of faith sprang into being. The truth about Jesus Christ, the crucified and risen Savior, was blessed to many hearts. Sinners everywhere turned from their sins and confessed Christ as Lord. God was working mightily, and the effects were clearly visible.

For the most part, the apostles were not well-educated men. Most of them grew up in the small villages of Galilee, learning trades such as fishing, building, and tax collecting. The religiously orthodox elite looked down on Galilee as a motley and compromised area, and indeed, much pagan darkness reigned there. The miserable effects of sin were visible everywhere: armies came and pillaged the land; demons possessed people; fear, disease, and death seemed to have the upper hand. And yet it was from this despised area that the author of the epistle of James came.

Meet James

Who was this James? James was a popular name at the time, so it shouldn't surprise us that more than one person with that name is mentioned in the Gospels. In the circle of the twelve apostles, two men were named James (Mark 1:19; 15:40). But it is generally accepted that it was not one of those two men but James, a half brother of Jesus, who wrote this short epistle. This man is mentioned in places such as Mark 6:3. He was a leader in the early church and was known as one of its pillars (Gal. 2:9). We meet this same James in the book of Acts, where he clearly has a place of prominence and authority. Scholars who have studied James's speech in Acts 15:13–21 have noticed a remarkable similarity between its language and style and that of this epistle. Early Christians, then, would have understood the simple reference to "James" in the first verse of this epistle to have been this James, the apostle.

Although James was privileged to grow up in the same home as the Lord Jesus, we are told that during Jesus's public ministry, James did not believe in Him (John 7:5). It is sobering to think that as "Jesus increased in wisdom and stature, and in favour with God and man" (Luke 2:52), James saw no beauty in Him that he should desire Him. After Jesus's resurrection, however, He made a special appearance to James (1 Cor. 15:7). This meeting is generally believed to have been the turning point in James's life, leading to his conversion. Now James could say with Paul: "Though we have known Christ after the flesh, yet now henceforth know we him no more" (2 Cor. 5:16). In other words, the human and physical tie between James and Jesus was not nearly as important as the spiritual tie between them. The Lord Jesus Christ was now his Lord and Savior.

After his conversion, James united with the company of believers who waited for the coming of the Spirit (Acts 1:14). He became a man of prayer, a leader in the church, and the author of this New Testament letter. He also shows himself to be an able shepherd of souls. A shepherd of souls is someone who has the mind and heart of the Lord Jesus, who is the Great Shepherd of souls (1 Peter 2:25; 5:2). A shepherd of souls shows the way, exposes dangers, feeds with truth, and leads weary sheep to quiet streams.

Scattered Sheep

James was writing from Jerusalem, and he addresses his epistle to the "twelve tribes which are scattered abroad" (1:1). This probably means he was writing to Jewish Christians who had been scattered throughout Israel and beyond. Because of the Assyrian and Babylonian exiles that had occurred long before James wrote, the Jewish people had already been scattered far and wide. Even when some Jews had returned (Ezra 1:4–6), most continued living outside of Palestine. We refer to this as the "Diaspora," which literally means the "scattering" or "sowing" of the Jewish people throughout the world. But there was also a more specific scattering of Jews that occurred during the time of the apostles. We read of this in Acts 8:1. Because of the persecution the early church faced at the hands of the Sanhedrin and other authorities, Christians had to flee for their lives.

Though we can't be certain about the exact date James wrote his epistle, most scholars believe that it is an early writing, perhaps the earliest part of the New Testament. For one thing, the book depicts a time of persecution, poverty, and oppression, characteristics of the earliest stage of apostolic Christianity.

Also, there are no references or allusions in the letter to matters pertaining to the Synod of Jerusalem, which took place in AD 48 or 49, as described in Acts 15. Bringing the gospel to the Gentile world brought with it many challenges, and this matter would have been a point of discussion at the Synod. James makes no mention of these challenges in his epistle, however, or of any tensions between Jews and Gentiles. This would lead us to believe the book predates the wide-scale spreading of the gospel to the Gentiles, which began in the late AD 40s. So although I can't say with total certainty, I believe James's letter was written during the first generation of Christianity after Pentecost, probably in the early AD 40s.

Conflict

A careful reading of James highlights another important part of the circumstances in which the earliest readers of this epistle found themselves. James frequently mentions the division and oppression within the community itself. The rich and the poor were at odds (2:6–7); the rich were oppressing the poor (5:4–6); and there was favoritism for the rich and disdain for the poor (2:1–4).

Conflict is always difficult, especially when people groups are set against each other. In this case, the "haves" and the "have nots" were at odds (5:1–6). No wonder James refers to dissensions (4:1–3) produced by selfish ambition and warns about the misuse of the tongue (3:1–12), since these were times characterized by such conflict.

James faults the rich for oppressing the poor and not paying proper wages to their workers (5:4–6). But the people James was writing to also had a worldly spirit (4:1–4), and though it may be easier to be worldly when you are rich, you can be just as obsessed with the world if you focus on what you don't have and want to get. James instructs the poor, then, to be patient (5:7–8).

Temptations

No doubt there were other trials and temptations these early Christians were facing, just as we face an amazing variety of challenges in our day. James opens his letter by referring to "divers temptations" (1:2), or various kinds of trials. Notice that James seems to use the words "temptations" and "trials" interchangeably. In 1:2, he writes of the Christians falling into "temptations." In 1:12, he speaks of enduring "temptation," but he also refers to being "tried." Perhaps you wonder what the difference is between trials and temptations.

Our difficulty in understanding these terms comes partly from our English language, in which the word "temptation" has a more negative connotation than "trial" does. We think of temptations as opportunities presented to us that lead us into sin, while we think of trials as difficulties through which God calls us to walk. But let's keep in mind that James is using the word "temptation" more neutrally and has in mind what we think of when we think of "trials." In that sense, then, the words are interchangeable.

Even if we think of trials and temptations as different things, isn't it true that they often weave themselves together? Satan tempts, trying to get us to stumble and fall into sin. We can't blame God for such temptations. He neither is tempted nor tempts anyone like that. But God can use what Satan intends for evil for good in the lives of His people. We could say, then, that God allows those temptations to become trials in our lives to mature us, to refine our faith, and to bring glory to Him. Here we see that God is standing above Satan in every way, even by using Satan's power to turn evil into something good.

This tempting to sin is exactly what Satan tried to do to Christ when he tempted Him in the wilderness (Matt. 4:1–11). He wanted so desperately to get Christ to fall! But God allowed this trial and used this temptation in the wilderness to prepare His Son for His ministry and to be a sympathetic representative of His people (Heb. 2:18). Christ was tempted so that He would know how heavy these temptations can be and how to identify with us in our weakness.

Again, there are many kinds of temptations. We often think of the temptation to lust, to commit adultery, or to murder, for example. It is true that such temptations are real and strong. But we shouldn't allow ourselves to be distracted by such "grandiose" temptations and overlook the thousands of other opportunities to sin. There is no such thing as a small or insignificant sin, and if Satan can catch us off guard, so much the better for him. Let's remind ourselves to be on our guard against *all* sin. Think, for example, of the

temptation to complain or to be lazy. Think of the temptation to slander someone or to gossip about him or her. Think
of the temptation to lie, to doubt, or to be proud or angry.
Think of the temptation to hypocrisy, to blasphemy, to fear
man, or to be double-minded. Even mistrusting the goodness
of God or doubting our faith and our salvation are forms of
temptation that Satan can use to discourage us or to doubt
God's saving work.

Like scattered and weary sheep, the early church was a
ready prey for Satan, the furious serpent (Rev. 12:15). It is
truly a miracle that it survived the persecution from without and the sin within. We can ascribe this survival only to
Christ obtaining all power in heaven and on earth (Matt.
28:18). From heaven He rules over everything, protecting
His church and strengthening her.

A Letter from James!

Imagine yourself in one of the meetings of the early church.
An elder announces the receipt of a letter from James, Jesus's
half brother and a church leader from Jerusalem. It was a
general epistle meant for a wide and general audience. He
reads the letter aloud. Wouldn't hearing the words of this letter have impressed you? Imagine hearing these words for the
first time: "Count it all joy when ye fall into divers temptations" (1:2). Or these: "Hath not God chosen the poor of this
world rich in faith, and heirs of the kingdom which he hath
promised to them that love him?" (2:5). Or these: "Behold,
we count them happy which endure" (5:11).

These words must have had a powerful impact on
those who heard them. This was a letter of encouragement

to endure through trials and temptations. It was a letter of warning against dead faith. It was a practical letter, touching on topics such as the use of the tongue, wisdom, submission, and riches. Near its end, it spoke about healing the sick through anointing and prayer. Its hearers were reminded of Job and Elijah as good models of endurance and fervent prayer. And these weren't just the words of James, the half brother of Jesus. These were inspired words. James was the "servant of God and of the Lord Jesus Christ" (1:1). God was the one who was writing them through the hand of James. It was His word that would help and direct these early Christians. That word would show them both what God was doing and what He was calling them to do, especially as it focused on truly knowing God and His grace and serving to His glory.

Pastor James

When you ask people what the book of James is about, many will mention one or more of its main topics, such as faith and works or the tongue. Some might say it is about Christian living, since it deals with many practical issues. These things are true, and they are important elements of the book. But to boil it all down, the basic theme of this short epistle is the difference between pure religion and vain (or carnal) religion. Pure religion is a state of the heart, but, as James describes, works are an indicator of spiritual health. This makes Christianity practical for daily life. So James's teaching is very practical, as 1:26–27 illustrates: "If any man among you seem to be religious, and bridleth not his tongue, but deceiveth his own heart, this man's religion is vain. Pure religion and undefiled before God and the Father is this, To visit the fatherless and widows in their affliction, and to keep himself unspotted from the world."

James shows himself to be a wise pastor of souls in this epistle. His readers are tempted and tried Christians, but rather than dwelling on this or encouraging any sort of morbid introspection, he encourages them to be busy doing the work of the Lord. He wants them using their time, tongue, and talents in ways that bring honor to God.

Isn't it true that we often get sidetracked from what the Christian life is all about as we fret, despair, or look within ourselves? James understands that. And he knows that even though temptation can be discouraging, it cannot ultimately hurt a true Christian. Instead of being sidetracked during times of trial, believers need to be busy doing what God wants them to do. We need to be shining like lights in the world.

In the end, trials should be triggers that call us to identify with others undergoing trials, to empathize with those who are in need, and to bring the comfort we have experienced to others who are in distress. Think of every trial as a reminder to you of your duties. Talk to yourself about what it is that God commands you to do: let me visit the widows and orphans; let me keep myself unspotted from the world; let me use my tongue in a way pleasing to God; let me live in friendship and communion with God.

Pure Religion

James calls this all "pure religion and undefiled" (1:27). This is the real thing! We are reminded of David, who also desired pure religion. In Psalm 51, he prays, "Wash me thoroughly from mine iniquity, and cleanse me from my sin" (v. 2). David knows that God is not pleased with only the appearance of religiosity. He desires "truth in the inward parts" (v. 6), an honest and upright heart toward Him. No phoniness. No hypocrisy. No duplicity.

Why do we need encouragement to desire true religion? Sadly, we easily content ourselves with what has been called a "fig-leaf" religion. Adam and Eve covered their shame with fig leaves (Gen. 3:7), somehow imagining that God would accept them that way. Ever since, this has been our innate tendency. We are easily satisfied with something the Bible calls the "chaff" or "husk" of a religious profession (see, e.g., Ps. 1:4) as opposed to the "wheat" or "grain," which really matters. God is pleased not with *religious profession*, but with *true possession* of what He is seeking from us. We should ask ourselves these questions: Does my profession pass the test of possession? Have I been thoroughly washed and cleansed, and am I true within?

Because God is pure, He wants us to be pure. He wants our worship and life to be singly devoted to Him. By pure, we don't mean that believers will never sin. That won't be the case on this side of eternity. But we do mean that believers should not be two-faced. There should be a consistency between their outward life and their inner life. If this consistency is there, they won't need to wear a "mask" to make themselves look good. They won't need to hide from others what they are like inside. That is what the Pharisees were so good at doing. Christ explained that they were experts in cleaning up the outside of their lives, while inside they were full of extortion and excess (Matt. 23:25). How they needed

Christ's warning: "Cleanse first that which is within the cup and platter, that the outside of them may be clean also" (Matt. 23:26).

Knowing the Difference

Throughout his epistle, James contrasts pure religion and impure religion on many points. Pure religion, he says, comes down from God and is established in the heart by spiritual regeneration (1:17). Meanwhile, impure religion springs from the heart, which brings forth sin, and sin brings forth death (1:15). Pure religion arises from the engrafted word, which saves the soul (1:21). Impure religion proceeds from the wrath of man (1:20).

Pure religion is visible in our actions. We cannot have the Holy Spirit in us without living it out to the world around us. When we have a close connection to God and our hearts are being transformed to His image, we will shine as lights in a dark place. When we walk as Christ walked and live as He lived in our world, we are showing that we possess true religion. To be sure, impure religion always remains in us, and therefore corrupt fruit always mixes itself with good fruit. Don't believers often have to confess how impure the thoughts and intents of their hearts are? But by God's grace, His purifying work in believers will continue and prevail.

Pure religion, when tested, is patient, constant, and God-glorifying (1:2–18). Impure religion wavers, is unstable in everything, and fades away (1:2–18). Pure religion is faith working by love (2:14–26). Those who have it keep themselves unspotted from the world (1:27), don't treat people with prejudice (2:1–3), and bridle their tongues (3:5–12).

They humble themselves before God (4:6–10) and rely on Him (4:13–15). They know fervent prayer (5:13–20). Impure religion, in contrast, does not work (2:4–26). It promotes jealousy (3:14–16) and lusts (4:1–12) and is degenerate (5:5).

Pure religion shows itself to be true in the end (1:4) and leads to the peace in our hearts that God alone can give (3:18). It will bear precious fruit until the Lord comes again (5:7). At the judgment, impure religion will not stand (2:13). God will unmask and expose it. Those who are marked by an empty profession of religion fall into condemnation (5:12). Only pure religion saves us from death (5:20). God will recognize only His truth and work, and those who are marked by it will be lifted up (4:10). Meanwhile, impure religion will lead only to punishment, death, and destruction (4:12) with the devil and his hosts (4:7).

God—Light without a Shadow

One key to James's writing is understanding his doctrine of God. When people interpret this book as being only practical, they are missing something that is key in James's thinking. James has much to say about God. The doctrine of God is present in every verse of his writing in the sense that each one teaches us something of His character, something of His promises, or something of His calling to us. The following verses are examples:

- God generously gives wisdom (1:5).

- God gives a crown of life to those who love Him (1:12).

- As the Father of lights, God gives only good and perfect gifts (1:17).

- God gives spiritual life in regeneration (1:18).

- God has chosen people to a kingdom He has promised to give them (2:5).

- God shows His friendship to people like Abraham (2:23).

- God has made people after His own image (3:9).

- God gives grace to the humble (4:6).

- God shows compassion and tender mercy to suffering people like Job (5:11).

- God can raise the sick and forgive sin (5:15).

As we see from this list, God is all goodness. These and other references prove that uppermost in James's mind is the character of God as the constant, giving, and forgiving friend of those who trust and love Him. This fits well with the most powerful description James gives of God: "Father of lights, with whom is no variableness, neither shadow of turning" (1:17). God is a faithful, covenant-keeping God. He does not change from one moment to another, from one year to another, from one century to another. He is light and gives light. He is a giver of only good and perfect gifts. He cannot veer even a little from what He has promised and pledged. There are no dark spots in the great character of the God who is light. He is pure, undiluted, holy, faithful, and good.

Study Questions

1. What can you reconstruct about God's work in James's life from the following passages: Mark 6:3; John 7:5; Acts 15:13–21; 21:18–25; 1 Corinthians 15:7?

2. In the days of the early church, God didn't often choose especially gifted or educated people to work in ministry. What does this say about God's priorities?

3. Give an example from your own life of a time when trial and temptation came together.

4. How is joy in suffering possible? Have you seen this in the life of someone you know? How does this motivate you to face your trials differently?

5. If pure religion and impure religion are so mixed in a believer, why do you think James makes such a sharp distinction between them?

6. Why is the character of God such an important starting point for James and for any understanding of His works and ways?

Reservoir 1

THE TRUTH OF GOD

James 1

It often seems easier to get things wrong than to get them right. Isn't there far more space outside the bulls-eye of a target than inside it? A common expression says, "A miss is as good as a mile." Perhaps this is particularly true when it concerns God's truth and work. For every inch of truth, there seems to be the potential for a mile of error.

We often think of non-Christians as having misconceptions of biblical truth or as not recognizing it; indeed, this is true, for their minds have not been enlightened by the truth (1 Cor. 2:14). But Christians, remaining prone to error, often misinterpret and misapply the truth as well. Circumstances can cloud our judgment; inward instability can make us inconsistent; indwelling sin can lead us astray. Our failure to heed God's Word robs us of its truths and insight. We often misjudge ourselves, those around us, and even God Himself. These things can especially be a problem when we are going through difficulties. Trials can come over us like a dense fog, clouding our vision and making us lose our bearings.

No wonder James gives this loving warning: "Do not err, my beloved brethren" (v. 16).

Clouds over Our Mind

This was the experience of the Jewish Christians to whom James was writing. Keep in mind that they were being persecuted and scattered; many were poor and oppressed. Peter refers to these circumstances as a fiery trial of faith (1 Peter 1:7). In other words, experiencing these things was like being in a fiery furnace. In times of such intense testing, it is difficult to know what to think, what to say, or even what to pray. It is hard to think straight and to see things as they really are—and to know what to do next. Trials have a way of showing us the limits of our wisdom. We exhaust our options and come up empty. It is as if James anticipates this, for he advises, "If any of you lack wisdom, let him ask of God" (v. 5).

Trials not only reveal the limits of our wisdom; they also have a way of revealing the instability within us. One part of us seeks after God; another part of us pulls away from Him. One part of us hates sin; another part pursues it. This inner war is wearying. James explains that this instability comes from double-mindedness (v. 8). The literal word here is "double-heartedness," and it refers to the opposite of "whole-heartedness" or "single-mindedness." It is the disposition that makes you feel as if you are being pulled in two directions. At times this inner tug-of-war seems to break your heart in two.

Worst of all, there are times when we find fault with God. As we struggle to understand what is happening to us, it becomes easy to wonder why God would allow this to happen. We may ask this question openly, or we may think it secretly. We may wonder if God is being too harsh with us, or if He is punishing us for something, or if He is trying to ruin us, or if He is tempting us to sin. We may find it difficult to see a loving God behind our circumstances. It seems that some of James's readers may have been thinking in these ways about their trials, for James warns: "Let no man say when he is tempted, I am tempted of God" (v. 13).

Can you identify with this fog that can come over your mind and heart during trials? What can drive away these clouds and help us not to just sink down in indecision, bitterness, and self-pity? Thankfully, James points the way.

Light from God's Truth

When we lose our moorings during times of trial, what we need most is divine truth spoken powerfully to us. Nothing sheds light on trials, temptations, and tests like the Word of God does. The key is to focus on its truth rather than on the circumstances around us or the feelings within us. This focus is exactly what James is working toward in his epistle.

First, James sheds the light of God's truth on *what our attitude under trial should be*. He writes: "My brethren, count it all joy when ye fall into divers temptations" (v. 2). These are remarkable words. Don't we think during times of trial that joy is far away? But remember, James is speaking here as "a servant of God and of the Lord Jesus Christ" (v. 1), so he is not simply giving us his personal advice or opinion. This call to joy comes from the Lord Himself.

Nor is James saying here that trials are joyful experiences in and of themselves. He is not encouraging us to convince ourselves that difficult circumstances are *not* difficult. But he is urging us to be active in seeing trials as opportunities for joy. He is encouraging us to see them from a different vantage point, one that is not natural for us. We should look at trials from the perspective of their ends—the effects they are meant to achieve (v. 4). You will not find joy by simply focusing on the trial itself. You might as well try to get honey from a thornbush. But if you trace the path of trial to its proper end, the trial will become a beacon of joy. Or to use another image: follow the bee that stung you to its hive, and the honey you find there will sweeten the pain. This is the truth that James is bringing. He knows the believer needs patience, and he knows that patience is forced to grow amid ongoing difficulties. He is concerned that patience have its perfect work; that is, that patience grow deeply in the believer's heart and give an inward stability and maturity (v. 4).

This teaching may seem contradictory to our human thinking. How can something painful be sweet? How can something difficult be a joyful experience? But think of how the teaching of the Lord Jesus also seemed contradictory to human reasoning, for example, in His Beatitudes: "Blessed are the poor in spirit.... Blessed are they that mourn.... Blessed are the meek..." (Matt. 5:3–5). These are truths that confound our human understanding. In a similar tone, James points us to an attitude of joy in trial. "Count it all joy," he says, because you are blessed.

Second, James sheds the light of God's truth, which *gives us wisdom when we lack it.* He writes: "If any of you lack wisdom, let him ask of God, that giveth to all men liberally, and upbraideth not; and it shall be given him" (v. 5). In other words, when our sources of wisdom run dry, we can rely on God's unfailing truth. He is willing to give us wisdom if we ask Him for it. Isn't this amazing? Too few ever ask, for they would find the promise true: "It shall be given" (v. 5). Yes, we need to persevere in asking, study God's Word, and look away from human wisdom. We need faith to believe God's truth and embrace it no matter how difficult it might seem. But the main point is this: truth lies readily accessible in God, who gives generously. Isn't this encouraging? Our God is abundant in wisdom, and He loves to give liberally. Think of King Solomon, who asked for wisdom and received not only wisdom but also much more from this generous Lord (1 Kings 3:11–13). The One who created us knows our frame—He knows how frail and foolish we are, how much we need wisdom. And He is long-suffering, slow to anger, and patient, not like a parent or teacher who quickly scolds and finds fault. Shouldn't this drive us to Him to ask for wisdom?

Third, James gives us God's truth *on various circumstances of life*. God calls His people to go through all sorts of experiences. But whatever we face, God's Word has guidance for us. If a Christian is poor, the truth James teaches is, "Let the brother of low degree rejoice in that he is exalted" (v. 9). If a Christian is rich, James has a truth for him as well: let him remember that his life will soon pass away (v. 10). Notice how James echoes the teaching of the Lord Jesus in the Sermon on the Mount. Christ warned against taking confidence in worldly treasures (see Matt. 6:19) and encouraged a humble trust in God for all the provisions of life (see Matt. 6:25–34). How we need God's truth to put our lives into proper perspective! We are so easily led to faulty conclusions from our circumstances rather than getting our perspective from His Word.

Finally, James uses truth *to correct wrong views of God*. As we saw earlier, a person whose mind is clouded might be inclined to blame God. But James reminds us of the truth: "God cannot be tempted with evil, neither tempteth he any man" (v. 13). James is reminding us that we can trust God. We would be miserable if left to believe that God was tempting us to sin. Instead, James puts the blame squarely on its source: "Every man is tempted, when he is drawn away of his own lust" (v. 14). Man can't be trusted, but God can. God sends down only perfect gifts (v. 17). What a faithful God!

The Truth about God's Character

This is a point worth emphasizing. When we are experiencing trials, we often imagine God to be withholding from us, as if He were stingy, difficult to please, and reluctant to give. At the bottom of a lot of pain in our lives is blindness to the unchanging character of God. If we knew His character better, we would have a mighty weapon of defense against the devil's whispers. We could find great comfort in our distress. We would have a pleading ground for prayer. We would have reason for hope and expectation, no matter what our circumstances are, for God's character is always the same, and His promises are steadfast and unchangeable.

On the other hand, when we doubt the truth about God's character, our source of strength dries up. We find ourselves with no available defenses against Satan's attacks. This is not to say that it is easy to always think rightly about God and His ways. We often struggle with unanswered questions, or our circumstances seem to contradict God's promises. We need to be realistic that this is something to which our human nature is prone. It is encouraging to remember that the writers of the Psalms often struggled with these things. They found themselves in low places and in tempting situations. At times, they even questioned God. Asaph complains in Psalm 73: "Verily I have cleansed my heart in vain, and washed my hands in innocency. For all the day long have I been plagued, and chastened every morning" (vv. 13–14). His faith was under attack, and he wondered whether it had all been worth it. It seems, humanly speaking, as if he was ready to give up. In Psalm 77:3 he writes, "I remembered God, and was troubled: I complained, and my spirit was overwhelmed." David also struggled with these kinds of questions. There were times when he felt forsaken by the Lord. He says in Psalm 13:1: "How long wilt thou forget me, O LORD? for ever? how long wilt thou hide thy face from me?" He complains in Psalm 42:9: "I will say unto God my rock, Why hast thou forgotten me? why go I mourning because of the oppression of the enemy?" Even the man after God's own heart said these things!

Expressing our feelings honestly is important in the life of faith. If we keep them bottled up in our hearts, they will fester. Bitterness will creep in, and happiness will seep out. But if we confess them honestly to God, who knows all the thoughts of our hearts anyway, we are taking them to the right place. Picture it like this. Sometimes our hearts are so full of complaining and unbelief that we can't fit any other kind of thought. We may be sitting under preaching or reading God's Word, but nothing seems to stick. There is just too much going on inside! But when we unburden ourselves in prayer to God, our hearts are at least partially emptied of their doubts and discouragements. Then there is room for other thoughts, for the truth about God, to enter.

And James tells us the truth that is so different from what we often think, especially when we are going through difficulties: God is a generous giver. He has said it in verse 5 (He "giveth to all men liberally"), and he repeats it in verse 17: "Every good gift and every perfect gift is from above, and cometh down from the Father of lights." Often we learn later, after an affliction has lessened or passed, that God was giving us many things before, during, and after the trial—gifts we weren't able to see at the time. How helpful it is to hear what James and other parts of Scripture reveal about God's character to us—how faithful, how generous, how bright He is! When God's Spirit applies this truth to us in the midst of our trials, our faith is strengthened. We can move more confidently and thankfully through our difficulties as we focus on the character of God.

A Love for Truth

Do you love the word of God and receive it deep into your heart? Everyone in whose heart God has worked loves and needs the word. After all, that word has made them new. The word of God is the instrument God uses to re-create fallen sinners. In unique circumstances, God can work without His word, such as when He regenerates children in the womb (see, e.g., Jer. 1:5) or a severely handicapped person who cannot hear or understand anything. God is able to do whatever He pleases. But it is His common way to use His Word to regenerate sinners. James reminds us of this when he writes, "Of his own will begat he us with the word of truth" (v. 18). God's truth was a powerful means in your regeneration, child of God. Shouldn't you hang on that word now, in your trials as well?

Actually, loving and receiving the word with humility is a sure indicator of whether God has worked in our hearts. James makes that clear just a few verses later: "Receive with meekness the engrafted word, which is able to save your souls" (v. 21). He is saying that we have a special connection with the word if things are right with us spiritually. We love to hear it and heed it, and we hide it in our hearts. It is engrafted, as it were, into our lives and becomes part of us. It molds and shapes us and helps us stay focused in trials. That doesn't mean we always value the word as we should; there are forces at work to pull us away from its truth. James lists the pollution ("filthiness") and wickedness ("naughtiness") of the world that are all around and which our flesh still desires (v. 21). Nevertheless, the word of God will triumph in the lives of God's people, not just at the beginning to regenerate them but from then on to sanctify, strengthen, and steady them.

The Touchstone of Truth

Long ago, when people working with metal needed to check whether it was genuine, they would scrape a hard stone, called a touchstone, across it. Genuine metal wouldn't be hurt by such a swipe, but something less than real metal might crumble or scratch. The stone would prove the authenticity of a genuine precious metal.

God's word is a kind of divine touchstone. It can be used to gauge the reality and authenticity of things. But sadly, so often we look to our circumstances as our touchstone. We think that if things are going well with us, God is favoring us; if things are not going well, we feel that He is displeased with us. No wonder we become confused, for we are using the wrong standard. The visible so often contradicts the invisible. As the saying goes, "Things are not always what they seem." Our circumstances don't give a complete picture of reality. We need to look past *external circumstances* to *eternal realities* as they are taught in the Scriptures. And when we do that, God makes us look away from things around us and causes us to focus on the truth of His word. That word sheds light on our lives and on our hearts. It acts as a touchstone, and it reveals whether or not God's grace is at work in our lives. No wonder James exclaims: "Do not err, my beloved brethren" (v. 16). It is so important that we use the right touchstone!

To put it simply: When God has worked in our souls, then we are not just hearers of the word, but doers thereof (vv. 22–23). Truth has formed us and continues to feed us. We live by it, not just in fair-weather times but also when the going gets tough, in trials and temptations. We live by it when people are watching but also when people aren't watching. We live by it when "important" people, who might reward us, need us, but we also live by it when those who might not be able to reward us—like widows and orphans (v. 27)—need us. And when we are doers of God's word by God's grace, we show to the world and also to our own hearts that God's truth is prevailing in our lives, and we are not deceiving ourselves for eternity. This powerful operation of truth in our lives can help us immensely. Then trials and temptations really do work for good to confirm us, to exercise God's grace in us, and to lead us to greater maturity and steadfastness, all by God's grace.

Self-Deception

James is keenly aware of the danger of self-deception; he writes about those who deceive their own hearts, who hear the word but do not do accordingly (v. 22). This is something to which all of us are prone as sinful human beings. Isaiah gives us this vivid picture of man by nature: "He feedeth on ashes: a deceived heart hath turned him aside, that he cannot deliver his soul, nor say, Is there not a lie in my right hand?" (Isa. 44:20). So we need something beyond ourselves that will help us not to err: something that will guide us into truth—and the truth about ourselves. Just being religious is not enough. People might speak in a way that sounds religious, but their tongues are deceptive. They might attend church and hear the word but not really receive it. They might be known as religious or spiritual people but still be attached to the world. Who will help us discern truth from error, the real from the false? God does through His word. James applies that touchstone in the following specific areas in these verses.

- *How we use our tongue*: James will say more about the tongue in chapter 3, but here already he highlights the importance of its proper use. An unbridled tongue can be evidence of a self-deceived heart (v. 26). Instead, he urges us to "be swift to hear, slow to speak, slow to wrath" (v. 19).

- *How we respond to the word*: The self-deceived are quickly finished with God's word. For them, reading the Bible is like a quick glance in the mirror. They adjust a few externals and are on their way, soon forgetting what they have read and failing to understand the Bible's deeper message. On the other hand, the godly look into "the perfect law of liberty"; far from being forgetful, they seek to put the word into practice (v. 25). They receive the word with meekness, and it is as if the word is engrafted, or rooted, into their very being (v. 21).

- *How we move through this world*: Impure religion has no problem immersing itself in the world; it feels most at home there. And the world's influence only further contaminates and weakens it. Its impurities correspond to the world's impurities. On the other hand, the believer seeks, by the grace of God, "to keep himself unspotted from the world" (v. 27).

Although it is not easy, self-examination is critical; the Bible calls us to it (2 Cor. 13:5). Perhaps as you are reading this, you fear you are deceiving yourself and that your religion is indeed vain. If that is so, I urge you to take another look at the second area to which James applies the touchstone of the word: how we respond to the word of God. How we respond when convicted by God's word reveals something about the state of our heart. It is not a good sign if we brush away and smooth over our convictions, for that is like we are looking into the mirror and refusing to acknowledge what we see. Instead, we should run to the God who is speaking in His word and seek His cleansing power in Jesus Christ. Through the Holy Spirit's work, He can give us honesty before Him and lead us to see our need for the cleansing blood of Christ, through which our sins can be forgiven. God's word vouches for His willingness to do this for needy sinners. Don't forget that James's advice in this chapter is to "ask in faith, nothing wavering" (v. 6). Pray for the grace to do that when you are convicted of your sins in a fresh way!

Reservoir of Truth

We have seen so far that God's truth is a real reservoir of strength in the midst of trial. It does at least three things according to James 1. First, truth drives away the clouds that hover over our life, bringing confusion and darkness, by helping us to see God's character and His wisdom, generosity, and faithfulness, which strengthens immensely. Second, truth sheds light on God's work in believers, assuring them and giving them stronger confidence through trials. Third, truth directs us and energizes us to do God's will with fresh vigor and resolve, even in affliction, and, for example, to help others in affliction, like widows and orphans, and thus be doers of the word.

Perhaps you are in the throes of temptation and trial right now, and the devil and his power seem very strong. Truth feels far away, and God's promises out of reach. Maybe you feel like the darkness has conquered you, that God has forsaken you and left you on your own. But there is one thing you can know for sure if you are a true believer. The unchangeable God cannot be unfaithful to His character or to His promises. Cling to the truth of the word of God, for it is a strong foundation on which to build. Without it, you are left to yourself and to the darkness of your erring heart. But if you submit to the word of God, you will have truth on which to rely, regardless of your circumstances. You will have access to joy, regardless of the sorrows you are facing. Christ will help you face every trial and every circumstance and turn it all to good (Rom. 8:28). So learn by grace to count it joy when you suffer trials and temptations. Don't rest until you draw strength from the reservoir of truth.

Study Questions

1. So often we think of trials as something we need to endure, which adds a note of passivity to them. What *active* behaviors does James recommend in times of trial (vv. 2, 3, 9, 12, 19–27)?

2. Verses 6–8 speak about doubt. Why is doubting such a serious insult to God? How does doubt affect our prayers?

3. In verse 13 James addresses our tendency to have negative thoughts about God. Give some other examples of wrong thoughts you might have had about God. Why are these so harmful to spiritual life? What can we do to combat them?

4. How can we keep ourselves unspotted from the world? Is this even realistic? Give some practical suggestions.

5. Why don't we see more people wanting to know whether they are deceiving themselves? How might you counsel someone who fears he or she is self-deceived and perhaps not a Christian at all?

6. Although honest self-examination is critical, is there a danger in self-examination that focuses too much on the sin within us? Why is it also important to focus on the promises of God and the work of Christ?

7. Think about difficult circumstances in the life of someone you know (or even in your own life). How can the reservoir of truth strengthen them and give hope?

Reservoir 2

THE LORDSHIP OF CHRIST

James 2:1–13

Many of us may remember a time in life when we enjoyed smooth, fair-weather sailing—when it seemed as though the sky was the limit and we were invincible. Failures, disappointments, losses, and sickness were things that others had to endure, but we happily knew nothing of them. How do we tend to feel about ourselves during times like this? Although we might not recognize these things in ourselves, we are often filled with pride and prejudice when we are enjoying prosperous times. We tend to have an entitlement attitude, thinking that we are somehow above those who don't have what we have. It is so tempting for us to think that somehow we've earned the things that we have. And so our attitude toward those around us who suffer becomes proud disdain rather than sympathetic pity.

Those of us who live in a democratic society and enjoy many personal freedoms may find the idea of a caste or class system appalling and offensive. Being locked into a certain level of society from birth, with no opportunity for upward mobility, is something hard for many of us to imagine.

Should a person be limited by what his or her parents were? But we may be forgetting that, by nature, all of us tend to think of society in a stratified way. Don't we all imagine ourselves as "higher up the ladder" than some others we know? Don't we spend lots of time and energy pulling ourselves up and putting others down? We don't *really* believe that all of us are on the same level. Even in the church, despite all that Scripture teaches, we can act in a way that hardly reckons with the fact that before God, we are all sinners—not one of us is better than that. And if by grace we have been redeemed by Christ, how little we have to boast of! For it was only grace that made a difference, where there was otherwise no difference at all.

God often uses trials to bring us down off our perches, empty us of our pride and prejudice, force us to face our limitations, and show us that we are nothing special. This can be so good for us spiritually! It can also give us new eyes to see those around us who are also going through difficulties; by God's grace, we may become a channel of love and mercy to them in a way that we couldn't have been before.

Don't Give In to Prejudice

At the beginning of chapter 2, James addresses the problem of "respect of persons" (v. 1). Let's try to put ourselves into the scene that James describes in the opening verses. Imagine that two visitors come to a worship service at your church. One of them is stylishly and expensively dressed and clearly has considerable wealth at his disposal. The other is shabbily dressed and has obviously bottomed out financially. The question is, how do you treat each of these visitors? Do you treat them differently? Are you more drawn to the wealthy man, and do you reach out to him with welcoming and flattering words? On the other hand, do you keep your distance from the poor man, making him feel unwelcome? Do you feel as if you are doing him a favor by even tolerating his presence? If your behavior is influenced by the outward appearance of these visitors, you would have failed the test that James has outlined here.

James calls this sin "respect of persons," or partiality—being "partial in yourselves" (vv. 1, 4). When you show partiality, you see a person's external appearance or demeanor as an indicator of his or her spiritual value, and you treat that person accordingly. You think that what is on the outside gives a good idea of what is on the inside. And so you are influenced by things that may be deceiving and without any real value. An attitude of partiality does not mesh with true faith. James writes, "Are [ye] become judges of evil thoughts?" (v. 4). In asking this question, he is implying that judgments influenced by partiality are influenced by evil thoughts, whether we are conscious of them or not. This is not a characteristic of true faith!

One important lesson we can learn from James's test is that *small, momentary actions have large-scale implications.* A small, impulsive action can express a whole world of thought and be a quick snapshot of what is in the heart. Don't we often make snap judgments about people and act accordingly? Our eyes, our looks, our smiles or frowns, and our impulsive words say so much about how we perceive people. They can evidence a proud and disinterested heart just as easily as they can evidence a warm and loving heart. Even things we have trouble seeing in ourselves can become obvious to those around us, as our actions betray our heart's desires and motives. And what people around us cannot see, God can see. He knows the thoughts behind each of our actions. He knows our hearts inside and out.

Christ Is the King of Glory

James is keen to point out that *faith and favoritism don't mix*. He writes unequivocally: "Have not the faith of our Lord Jesus Christ, the Lord of glory, with respect of persons" (v. 1). What he means is this: If you truly believe on the Lord Jesus Christ, who is now exalted in heaven as the only Lord of glory, you cannot be carried away with any appearance of earthly glory—by riches, power, or prestige. Before Him, all of us are on the same level. Think of what Christ taught during His time on earth; He never taught a faith that judged by appearances. Quite the contrary! He was a friend of publicans and sinners (Luke 15:1–2). He warned against the Pharisees' judgment of people based on externals (Luke 16:14–15) and against cleaning the "outside of the cup" but not the inside (Matt. 23:25). He showed how poor Lazarus, who had to survive on crumbs, was carried to heaven, while the rich man, who died in his sins, ended up in hell (Luke 16:19–23). Should the followers of Christ turn the faith that He taught into favoritism, which He condemned?

What is more, the Lord Jesus was Himself once the Man of Suffering. Isaiah 53:3 says of Him, "He is despised and rejected of men; a man of sorrows, and acquainted with grief: and we hid as it were our faces from him; he was despised, and we esteemed him not." He was lowly and meek and took the form of a servant (see John 13:4 and Phil. 2:7), and He called His people to follow Him in serving others and in taking the lowest place. So respect of persons has no place in the kingdom of heaven. Its judgmental spirit is condemned by the gospel and is something of which Christians must be cured.

But James does not hesitate to show Christ in all His glory now as he calls Him, "Lord Jesus Christ, the Lord of glory" (v. 1). This Man of Suffering is now exalted above all principalities and powers (Eph. 1:21). He has a name above every name (Phil. 2:9). He alone is worthy of our respect and honor.

What does this mean for believers, practically speaking? Whatever your own trials are and whatever trials you haven't had to endure, don't harbor bitterness, prejudice, or racism against others. Instead, reach outside of yourself, even if you need to step out of your peer group or comfort zone to do so. Look beyond the externals, and try to focus on the person inside. Seek to be a blessing to others, as the Lord calls you to. Pray for an empathetic and sympathetic heart that enters into others' trials. Pray that your heart would be filled with God's love for others, and let little actions—a warm smile, eye contact, a friendly greeting, a considerate question—display that love. Study the life of our Lord Jesus as it is described in the Gospels, for He Himself has modeled that love for us.

We are all tempted to favor some people over others. We may be especially prone to this sin when our faith is at low ebb and we are not living in dependence on God's free grace. Don't we need to understand more of that grace, rely more on it, and display more of it to others? For grace has no favorites.

It accepts unworthy sinners freely, not on the basis of who
they are or what they have done. James wants his readers to
have, by grace, a strong faith that is unobstructed by ungodly
pride. So he highlights the toxic effects of harboring prejudice against others. He wants us instead to cast aside our
prejudice and reach out to people more disadvantaged than
we are. This will help us to grow in grace and make us more
like our Lord.

The King Is a King of Love

In verse 5, James asks, "Hath not God chosen the poor of
this world rich in faith, and heirs of the kingdom which he
hath promised to them that love him?" In other words, God
Himself chooses the most surprising sorts of people to be
His own. In general, it has not been the rich and famous
whom He has called to Himself; when you trace who God's
people have been throughout the ages, you find quite the
opposite. His people have been wandering patriarchs (Deut.
26:5), enslaved shepherds (Exodus 1–2), and poor widows
like Naomi and Ruth (Ruth 1). In each of these cases, God
showed mercy to those who were not highly esteemed by
society. Shouldn't this warn us against showing any kind of
partiality or prejudice? But sadly, the church often does the
opposite of what God has done.

James warns of the toll taken on the witness of Christians when they do not follow their Lord's example and show
gospel love for poor sinners. He asks, "Do not they blaspheme
that worthy name by the which ye are called?" (v. 7). In other
words, people are pointing their fingers at Christians, notic-
ing how they treat each other. The rich are favored, and the

poor are despised, even among believers and in the church. This gives unbelievers an excuse to blaspheme the gospel. And as they ridicule and mock *Christians*, James says, they are mocking and ridiculing the One whose name Christians are carrying: *Christ*. Does the Lord of glory deserve that? It is a contradiction for those who bear the name of Christ to act differently than He did. Christians are to be Christ's body on earth, to be salt and light. What a sobering reminder! Shouldn't mercy, love, and compassion shine through in our lives and in how we treat each other?

The Kingdom Is a Kingdom of Love

James carries his teaching further by speaking about the second table of the moral law, which he calls "the royal law" (v. 8). He means to show that prejudice or favoritism goes directly against what God demands in His law.

What is God's will for His people? James makes this clear in verses 8–13. He writes, "If ye fulfil the royal law according to the scripture, Thou shalt love thy neighbour as thyself, ye do well" (v. 8). So God's law demands love for our neighbor. The law is not a code for external behavior only. It is not only about dos and don'ts. *Love* is the fulfillment of the law. This means both love for God *and* love for our neighbor, the two being intrinsically connected. As 1 John 4:20 says, "If a man say, I love God, and hateth his brother, he is a liar: for he that loveth not his brother whom he hath seen, how can he love God whom he hath not seen?" But James's specific focus in these verses is the necessity of showing love to our neighbor.

Think about God giving the Ten Commandments at Mount Sinai. He gave this law to a poor band of slaves, the children of Israel, whom He had freed from their captivity in Egypt. He took them for His people and established His kingship from the outset: "I [am] the LORD thy God" (Ex. 20:5). That is why this law is called a "royal law" (v. 8) and a "law of liberty" (v. 12). It is given by a King who sets His people free from sin and calls them to a life of obedience.

You certainly cannot claim the law on your side if you act with partiality. In fact, in the judgment, you will be shown no mercy if you have not acted in mercy toward those around you (v. 13). God wants His people to reflect His character. That is His royal policy, and all His subjects learn to follow it. If you judge people with evil thoughts now, God will judge you with evil thoughts. And to all those who reach out in mercy and righteousness from out of the strength God gives, the Lord Jesus says: "Inasmuch as ye have done it unto one of the least of these my brethren, ye have done it unto me" (Matt. 25:40).

We should remember that James is keen to show how trials test whether the faith that many people profess is genuine. Let's apply that thought here as well. We need to make sure we don't have the "faith" of the priest and the Levite, who made a wide circle around the man in need (Luke 10:31–32). Theirs was not a true faith. True faith will show itself in loving God and loving our neighbor, showing compassion to those in need. James will continue dealing with this theme later in chapter 2, proving that faith without works is empty and vain.

The Reservoir of the Lordship of Christ
The lordship of Christ should challenge us to show His love for those around us, especially those who are suffering. It

should encourage us if we are going through trials ourselves. The Lord Jesus Christ draws us into a kingdom where those who are weary and worn are welcomed. This is not a kingdom in which the poor are further beaten down and only those with status are prized. All are on equal footing, saved only by grace. Notice that in verse 5 of this chapter, James points out that both rich and poor are "heirs of the kingdom which he hath promised to them that love him." If we, by grace, have been brought to love Him who first loved us, we are the richest of all people!

James is also implicitly urging us not just to have a little faith, but to be "rich in faith" (v. 5), no matter how poor or tried we are. We will have such a faith if we look away from ourselves to the Lord Jesus Christ, the Lord of glory. We will have such a faith if we don't look to have glory, esteem, pomp, and prestige here but instead seek, with a lowly heart, the blessing and approval of Christ.

Perhaps you are going through great trials as you read this. In the past you may have been trying to build a little kingdom of your own here on earth. But now you realize that the trials the Lord has sent are designed to make you seek first His kingdom (Matt. 6:33). Look up then to the Lord of glory, content to wait on Him and to be a channel of His mercy to others. And pray to the Lord, like the disciples did, "Increase our faith" (Luke 17:5).

Study Questions

1. Why does the scene in verses 2 and 3 of this chapter still seem so realistic today, roughly two thousand years after James painted it? How can we make our churches different?

2. How big a problem do you think materialism is in our day? Does this hinder our witness to the world?

3. Look at the terms James uses for the moral law: "royal law" (v. 8) and the "law of liberty" (v. 12). Discuss the meaning of these terms. Why don't we think more of the moral law as a law of liberty?

4. How does the fact that Christ was once the lowly Servant and is now the glorious Lord (v. 1) put the suffering of His people into perspective?

5. Suffering can make us turn inward and focus on ourselves. Why is this section of James so helpful in directing us toward others who may be just as needy as or even needier than we are?

6. What does it mean to be "rich in faith" (v. 5)? How should we think of this in the midst of trials?

THE FRIENDSHIP OF GOD

James 2:14–26

When we go through difficult circumstances, we often find out who our true friends are. A true friend will stay with us through thick and thin—a rare but wonderful blessing! We find such comfort in being able to tell a friend what we're going through. Isn't it so often true that a burden shared is a burden halved? A friend's support, help, love, and prayers mean so much when we are in trouble. We can be vulnerable with true friends, because we are safe with them.

But it is when times get hard that a friend who is only interested in going through good times with us will drift away. The betrayal of a friend, just at the time when we need him or her most, can be painful. The Lord Jesus experienced this. One of the great agonies associated with His sufferings was when His friends forsook Him. Judas betrayed Him, as Christ knew he would. But His beloved friend Peter also denied that he knew Christ. And in the end, all His disciples ran away and were offended because of what He was enduring. How this must have added to Christ's sufferings! As a true human being, He also needed friends, and the Bible tells us that He enjoyed a special friendship with Mary, Martha, and Lazarus (John 11:5). How it must have touched His suffering heart that His beloved disciple John followed Him from afar and stood at the foot of His cross, along with a few women.

If a human friend is such a precious gift, how much more precious is friendship with God—and this is how the Lord is pleased to relate to His people. What better friend could believers have than their Lord Himself? With Him by their side, they are safe, regardless of their circumstances. This is the third reservoir of strength that James presents in the second half of chapter 2.

Subjects and Friends

We typically think that the main point of this section of James's epistle is the relationship between faith and works. Indeed, he has much to say about faith and works here. But we need to be careful not to miss the main purpose of James's writing. His purpose here is not to present some sort of theological treatise on the connection between faith and works; rather, it is to stress *the importance of having true faith*. If we, by grace, do have true faith, we will know the friendship of God (v. 23).

Remember that James is encouraging believers undergoing trials. He knows that the friendship of God can be a great source of strength, especially in difficult times, when we so often feel alone and bereft of human helpers. It is not a coincidence that the importance of friendship with God will be brought up again later in this epistle (see 4:4).

We saw in the first part of chapter 2 that God is a king of love who has chosen surprising sorts of people as His own

(2:5). In this part of the chapter, two of those people are named specifically: Abraham the idolater (v. 23) and Rahab the harlot (v. 25). These two sinners were brought into God's kingdom as both His subjects and His friends. Before we go any further, let's think about that. Isn't it simply astounding that God is willing to call sinners His friends? Isn't it amazing that those who become this king of love's subjects also become His friends? Yet it is possible, and it is true. God's design for friendship with fallen people originated in eternity past, when He purposed to draw sinners from among the fallen human race to Himself. These sinners wouldn't deserve friendship with the living God. They wouldn't be able to earn it from their side by their good works. It would be only through His Son, Jesus Christ, and His death on the cross that these sinners would be made His friends. Christ's sacrifice would pay the debt they owed and restore broken communion with God. Rebels would be drawn with strong bonds of love, would be reconciled, and would become friends. What amazing, undeserved grace!

Trust in Action

So what do faith and works have to do with friendship, practically speaking? Why does James even bring the idea of friendship with God into this chapter (v. 23)? Let's think for a moment about what faith is. True faith, as it is described in Scripture, includes knowledge, assent, and trust (or confidence). Trusting God and His word is absolutely crucial in the life of faith.

We would all agree that trust is an important ingredient in friendship. You wouldn't want a close friendship with someone you didn't trust, would you? And trust isn't just a nice thought that two friends assume is part of their relationship; it shows itself in actions and helps the friendship grow. And what is true on a human level is also true on a spiritual level. You aren't a friend of God if you don't trust and confide in Him. And you aren't a friend of God if this trust doesn't show itself in obedience to God and His word. In John 15:14, Jesus says to His disciples, "Ye are my friends, if ye do whatsoever I command you."

To help us understand the importance of works to prove that someone's faith is genuine and true, James introduces this idea of dead faith in contrast to genuine or true faith. He gives two examples to illustrate what he means by dead faith. First, dead faith is like a man who speaks but doesn't act (vv. 15–16). He sees people in need but can't muster more than a few words to wish them well. Are such words going to accomplish anything? No, they are empty and vain, just like dead faith is.

The second illustration of dead faith is the faith of the devils (v. 19). They believe and even tremble, but are they saved? Of course not! Their unrighteous actions prove that their believing and trembling are in vain. How sobering to think that there may be people in church who have only the faith equivalent of the faith of devils. How important that we ask ourselves these questions: Do I have a faith that is only words but no actions? Do I have only a devil's faith? Or do I have the true faith of a friend of God?

Trust in Trial

In these verses, James wants to focus on how trust shows itself in action in the midst of trials. Remember, James wants to strengthen believers who are facing trials. He doesn't want Christians to be driven to doubt and despair by difficult circumstances; he wants them to test the reality of their faith in the midst of trying circumstances. He wants them to exercise themselves in the work and for the cause of God, obeying His will even in trials; as they do so, their faith in Him will prove itself to be true. Trials can never destroy a trust that has its source in God; on the contrary, God will open up more and more of His heart of friendship to those who go forward in obedience.

This line of reasoning makes sense of the two examples James gives here—Abraham and Rahab. Both of them exercised faith in the midst of a great trial. James points us first to Abraham, who was asked by God to offer up to Him his only son, Isaac (Gen. 22:1–2). Think for a moment about what God's command must have meant for Abraham. God was asking him to give up his only son, his promised son! I am amazed that Abraham wasn't frozen into immobility by confusion and questioning, for that is what I expect would happen to me in such a situation. Instead, Abraham went forward in faith and obedience, preparing to sacrifice Isaac. His friendship with God was shown to be unshakeable, strong, and rewarding. His faith shone brightly. In the end, God confirmed his faith from heaven (v. 23), and Isaac was spared. What encouragement this should be to believers who are in trial! God will confirm your faith if you live in obedience to Him and in friendship with Him.

Rahab was another tried Old Testament believer. Her story, which you can read in Joshua 2, is amazing, considering that she was from a heathen nation and had been taught little about the God of Israel (Josh. 2:1–22). As a Canaanite harlot, doesn't she seem a most unlikely candidate for friendship with God? The Canaanites were under God's judgment and curse because of their iniquity. But God had mercy on Rahab, bringing her into relationship with Himself and making her a remarkable monument of His grace.

Rahab had heard reports about Israel's God, and, as she told the Israelite spies, she had believed what she had heard. She acknowledged that God was the only God and that He alone could save. She desired to be shown the kindness of this God. Despite the many challenges her young faith faced—the risks of hiding the spies, being questioned by the king, waiting in suspense for the Israelites to come, wondering whether the scarlet cord would save her—the Lord brought her through. Rahab was not put to shame (v. 25). She went on to become a mother in Israel and was in the line of Jesus Christ (Matt. 1:5).

Let's use this opportunity to examine ourselves. Is God our friend? Do we have true faith? If so, does our trust in Him show itself to be real, especially in trials? Do we press on in obedience to God, even when things get difficult? Does the empty hand of our faith draw from God's friendly heart toward us grace after grace after grace?

Be Fruitful in Faith

Some people become confused when they read these verses in chapter 2. They think that James is contradicting what the apostle Paul teaches about faith, works, and justification. Doesn't Paul clearly teach that we are saved by faith alone, without the deeds of the law, and that faith alone justifies (e.g., Rom. 4:5)? Indeed, he does. But there is no contradiction between Paul's teaching and James's emphasis in these verses. Paul teaches that works done before or alongside faith can contribute nothing to justification; this justification involves *being declared righteous in the eyes of God* on the basis of the righteousness of Jesus Christ, received with the empty hand of faith. James, on the other hand, emphasizes that true faith will show itself by the works that flow from it. He uses the word "justified" in verses 21, 24, and 25 in the sense of being proven before people. What James means is this: A bare profession of belief should not be mistaken for saving faith. True faith is more than a mere assent to certain doctrines. The works that follow true faith will prove it to be real. In that sense, a believer is "justified" by his or her works. This is what Abraham's and Rahab's works did (see vv. 23, 25). So Paul's teaching and James's teaching mesh together perfectly.

None of us should rest content without this true faith, which manifests itself in actions. Martin Luther wrote:

> Oh, it is a living, busy, active, mighty thing, this faith; and so it is impossible for it not to do good works incessantly. It does not ask whether there are good works to do, but before the question rises, it has already done them, and is always at the doing of them. He who does not these works is a faithless man. He gropes and looks about after faith and good works, and knows neither what faith is nor what good works are, though

he talks and talks, with many words, about faith and good works.[1]

Reservoir of Friendship

Perhaps as you read this, you or someone you love is in the midst of a trial. Friends may have let you down, and you feel completely alone. Or perhaps after reading about faith and works, you feel like whatever faith you thought you had is empty and vain. It has all been a delusion!

When you feel discouraged like this, remember that God calls His friends those who trust Him fully, even when circumstances are hard. He wants to strengthen His people and reveal more of His friendship to them, like He did to Abraham and Rahab in their trials. The Son of God came down and suffered many afflictions so that He could be the sympathizing Friend who sticks closer than a brother (Prov. 18:24). He came so close to us. Isn't He the best friend you could wish for? His wisdom, His love, His forgiveness, and His comfort give you more than any earthly friend could ever give you. You can walk with Him in firm trust, day by day. And when earthly friends leave you, when you feel alone in a trial, or when you are unable to be a good friend yourself, your Friend will be there to help and encourage you. He will never leave or forsake you. The friendship of God—another deep reservoir of strength!

---

1. Martin Luther, *Commentary on Romans*, trans. J. Mueller (Grand Rapids: Zondervan, 1954), xvii.

Study Questions

1. How are true friends helpful when we are going through difficulties? What can strain our friendships during difficult times?

2. Abraham was called a friend of God. What does this say about the kind of relationship God wants with us? How do we become God's friends?

3. How important is prayer if we have God as our friend?

4. Why do you think James uses Abraham and Rahab as examples in this chapter? How do we see faith shining in the midst of their trials?

5. In the parable of the sower (Mark 4:1–8), Christ teaches that troubles make some fall away from the faith. How do trials distinguish the real from the false?

6. Though believers are justified by faith alone, why can faith never remain alone (v. 17)?

7. Job was accused of being a hypocrite (see Job 22:21–30). Apply what you've learned in this chapter about faith, trust, obedience, works, and friendship to his situation. How could you prove this accusation wrong?

THE WISDOM OF GOD

James 3

Trials often bring us to the end of our own wisdom. Things we thought we had a hold on may seem to escape us when we need them most. Things we thought we understood don't seem to make sense anymore. Things we said to comfort or help others when they were experiencing a trial may sound like hollow truths when we are going through something ourselves. How quickly we may find ourselves at the end of our resources and in desperate need of wisdom!

The book of Job speaks powerfully to the subject of suffering. At times Job was able to express his faith brightly in the midst of his troubles (e.g., Job 1:21; 13:15; 19:23–27; 23:8–10). But Job and his friends struggled to make sense of what he was going through. Each of them had his own opinions and interpretations, but in the final analysis wisdom eluded them all; they were unable to explain what Job was enduring. Job came to realize that and wrote in chapter 28: "But where shall wisdom be found? and where is the place of understanding? Man knoweth not the price thereof; neither is it found in the land of the living" (vv. 12–13).

Then, in chapters 38–42, God spoke. Job was convicted that he had spoken rashly. He confessed in 40:4–5: "Behold, I am vile; what shall I answer thee? I will lay mine hand upon my mouth. Once have I spoken; but I will not answer: yea, twice; but I will proceed no further." In chapter 42 he said: "I have heard of thee by the hearing of the ear: but now mine eye seeth thee. Wherefore I abhor myself, and repent in dust and ashes" (vv. 5–6). Listening to God, Job had begun to realize how small he was and how little he knew. He now knew that much of what he had said was not right. God's wisdom had shed new light on his situation and taught him things he had not known before.

Sadly, it does not seem that Job's three friends learned the same lessons. God rebuked them sharply, saying to Eliphaz, "My wrath is kindled against thee, and against thy two friends: for ye have not spoken of me the thing that is right, as my servant Job hath" (Job 42:7). Perhaps the three of them should have kept up the silence that they had resorted to early on, for their speeches did not betray true wisdom. What a reminder to us that we should be careful about offering explanations for trials that others are going through!

And so it is fitting that, in the context of undergoing trials, James opens this chapter with a warning against being "many masters" (v. 1), since we offend in so many ways, including in our speech (v. 2). We need to be so careful not to act as if we understand God's ways perfectly and can speak to what He is doing. Speaking rashly is always dangerous, but especially so when we, or others, are facing difficult circumstances. How we need the wisdom that is from above

(v. 17) at all times, for that wisdom will impact our speech in a God-honoring way.

Our Tongue

The Puritans called pastors physicians of the soul. That is true, for a faithful pastor seeks to diagnose what ails people spiritually. And, as we've noted, James is a wise pastor in this epistle. He has already "checked" our eyes, probing whether we show favoritism based on how people appear. Now he focuses on our speech, as he deals with the tongue.

The tongue is truly a remarkable creation. In cooperation with air and the structures of our mouths, our tongues produce intelligible sounds that help us communicate. The thoughts of our minds and emotions of our hearts can be expressed to others through our tongues.

Because it is such a primary means of communication with others, the tongue makes for an interesting diagnostic tool; an analysis of what comes from our tongue can tell us whether we possess true wisdom. Looking at what we say over the course of a day, week, or more, we can learn much about the health of our inner being. Are we still in a state of uprightness before God, as we were when we were created? Or do we see grim evidence of our fallen nature in the words that we speak? Has our speech been sanctified through the work of the Holy Spirit in our lives? Are our thoughts and emotions in accord with His Word? Do we consistently edify each other and praise God with our tongues?

If we are honest, it should be easy for us to see how our tongues betray our sinful natures. Before their fall into sin, Adam and Eve said only things that were pleasing and glorifying to God. They had been made in His image, and their speech reflected that image. Their words were characterized by knowledge, righteousness, and holiness. The things they said to each other were always loving and appropriate. But their speech was radically transformed when sin entered into the world. The devil, the father of lies (John 8:44), promised that Adam and Eve could be as wise as God if they disobeyed His command. Giving in to Satan's temptation meant that Adam and Eve, and the human race that would follow them, also became liars. The human tongue is now one of the greatest instruments of evil in the world. You could say that it is the insignia of hell. It is difficult to imagine what a world free of sinful speech would look like. What a wonderful world that would have been!

Tongue Problems

Let's follow James as he takes a closer look at the tongue (vv. 3–12). First, what a *small but powerful* thing the tongue is (vv. 3–5a). James compares it to a bit in a horse's mouth, which is able to steer the animal's whole body (v. 3), or to the small helm on a large ship, which is able to maneuver the vessel both in calm seas and through storms (v. 4). Do we think often enough about the power of words? Do we realize how much our words are able to do? Our speech can have great influence in others' lives—with only a few words we can encourage them to do right, tempt them to do wrong, build them up, and break them down.

Second, the tongue is *small but destructive* (vv. 5b–6). James compares it to the match that starts a forest fire. In other words, a lot of damage can be done by a few words.

Watch how one tongue stokes the next tongue, which passes the flame on to the next. Soon, the world is ablaze with the fire that one tongue ignited. Where does this kind of fire come from? James does not mince words here; he says that the original spark came from hell (v. 6b). Unrestrained and unsanctified, the tongue can ruin lives and cause great distress. What a point for self-examination! What fires have our tongues ignited? Is our speech destructive? Does it devastate those around us? Or, as a result of the Lord's work of grace, are our tongues instruments of grace and healing in this broken world?

Third, the tongue is *small but untamable* (vv. 7–8). Often, something small is easily controlled. But that is not the case with the tongue. James writes, "The tongue can no man tame; it is an unruly evil, full of deadly poison" (v. 8). James contrasts the tongue with the beasts, birds, serpents, and sea creatures that have been tamed by humans. All of those animals have been subdued and brought under control through various techniques—but no such methods work on the human tongue. Positive and negative reinforcement and punishment fail to curb sinful speech, which continually erupts from a sinful heart.

Fourth, the tongue is *a source of contradiction* (vv. 9–12). Listen to someone speaking one moment, and you'll hear the most beautiful praises uttered to God. But what might we hear only a short time later? The same tongue may be cursing (v. 9). What extreme opposites! Where in nature has a water source been discovered that pours out fresh water and salt water interchangeably? Where is there a fig tree that produces figs one season and olives the next? The created world is an orderly one. But our speech betrays such contradictions. What a reflection of our hearts, which are so inconsistent!

James's analysis of the tongue yields these sobering descriptions. Notice how James has found parallels for the tongue in the world; it can be compared to a bit, a helm, and a fire (vv. 3–6). But it is as if the tongue goes beyond what is normal and natural in the created order, for it is unruly, untamable, and contradictory. It seems that when it comes to the evil of the tongue, even science must plead ignorance!

And, indeed, man's knowledge cannot cure the evil of the tongue. It might curb the evil a little bit and reform manners a tad, but none of this will be enough. Is it hopeless then? Thankfully, not. James goes on to describe a reservoir from which we can draw hope and healing, and this time the reservoir is the wisdom of God (vv. 13–17).

Wisdom from Above

James wants to be clear about what true wisdom is (v. 13). After all, there is a lot that passes for wisdom. Academic, scientific, and practical knowledge can help us up to a point and can be used for many good purposes in this world, but this kind of knowledge is limited in its scope and stained with sin. In the end, human knowledge falls short of the wisdom that we need to really address great and eternal realities. What Nobel Prize winner has been able to explain the problem with the human tongue, much less all the other misery in the world? Remember how Job's friends, who were wise people, were unable to explain his predicament. Their explanations failed, and God rebuked the friends.

If we immersed ourselves in the intelligence of this world, we would, for the most part, see quite the opposite of heavenly wisdom. We would find arrogance, prejudice, jealousy, and other sinful vices. This is what James is saying: such humanistic "wisdom" is born of envy, that proud ambition lurking in the depraved soul. Though it may look good on the outside, it is actually full of prejudice and hypocrisy (v. 17). Such wisdom can't escape its earthly, sensual, and devilish roots (v. 15). It manifests itself in disorderly confusion and evil practices (v. 16).

Where should we look for true wisdom? James is clear on this point too. Only *the wisdom which is from above can help us* (vv. 17–18). This wisdom not only helps us make sense of our problems; it can also solve them. It will address not only the evil of the tongue but the whole of our conduct (v. 13). James describes this wisdom for us in verses 17 and 18. It descends from above. It is, first, pure—not mixed or stained but holy and wholesome. In addition, it is characterized by peace, fairness, and mercy. It knows no favoritism or hypocrisy. It is humble and gentle and leaves in its wake a trail of righteousness like satisfying fruit, even through suffering.

Notice the connections to peace made in verses 17 and 18. Wisdom from above brings peace, for it has its source in the peaceful heart of God. God alone can give and bring peace through His Word and Spirit, and He can do so even in the most restless and tumultuous of circumstances. Have you ever met a person whose words seem to always have a calming effect in his or her relationships, even in difficult situations? Christ was the perfect example of a peacemaker. His words even calmed the wind and the waves as He said,

"Peace, be still" (Mark 4:39). That is what we could call "wisdom that is from above" (v. 17).

The Reservoir of Wisdom

Perhaps you wonder if there is hope for you. You realize how often you have misused your tongue. You have failed God, your family, your friends, and yourself. So often when you have lacked strength, you have drawn strength from your own reservoirs rather than seeking it from God. Failing to use your tongue wisely has done so much damage.

But, friend, there is hope! There is a reservoir full of divine wisdom. If our own reservoir of wisdom has dried up—or been dry for a long time—we can look to the reservoir that will never run dry. The wisdom in it has been there from eternity, in God, and it will last to eternity. God has all the wisdom we need, no matter how impossible the situation looks. When we cry to Him, it is like we are taking our empty buckets to the reservoir that is so full that all the buckets of the world couldn't empty it. There is no limit to His understanding (see Isa. 40:28).

God often uses suffering in our life to change us. Even the way we use our tongues can be sanctified through trial. Sometimes the answers we had at the tips of our tongues are taken away. Things we have parroted to the people around us become hollow and meaningless. We realize how often we have spoken with too much self-confidence. What a blessing to come to the end of our own wisdom! What a relief it is to rest in God, whose heavenly wisdom can renew us after the image of Christ, whom the Bible calls true Wisdom. What peace this brings to the chaos inside us! When Christ was on earth, people said of Him: "Never man spake like this man" (John 7:46). His speech betrayed His perfect wisdom. In His life and death, He sowed a harvest of righteousness that is most perfectly suited to atone for the sins of our tongues and to produce, through the Spirit of wisdom, all that we need for sanctification. When our minds are reshaped after the image of Christ, through His saving work, this wisdom grows. And again, a promise bubbles up in this reservoir, reminding us that whenever we need wisdom from above, it will be given to us.

Study Questions

1. What does verse 2 tell us about the importance of our speech? How does speech betray our true character?

2. What specifically does the tongue do, according to verses 6 and 8? Give examples of ways in which it does these things.

3. Why should we guard our tongues especially during trials? How can we do this?

4. What does it mean to bless God (v. 9) with our speech in daily life?

5. Why is the devil so invested in making us use our tongues in a way that projects badly on God and others? What are some examples of this from your life?

6. How are verses 10–12 an example of the double-mindedness (double-heartedness) that James mentioned in chapter 1?

7. Examine and explain the eight characteristics of true wisdom in verse 17. How can we obtain godly wisdom, and how can this wisdom change the way we communicate?

THE GRACE OF GOD

James 4:1–12

People are drawn to stories—something about them enthralls us. We wonder how the story will end, especially if there are heroes and villains involved. Will the right woman be with the right man when it is all over? Will there be a beautiful wedding? Will the hero be vindicated? Will the villain be brought to justice?

At one basic level, the Bible could be described as a great, dramatic love story. Its last book, Revelation, tells of a wedding feast that has been a long time in the making (chapter 21). It is the marriage supper of the Lamb with His bride, the church. The plot of this story is a complex one, with many twists and turns. There have been many dangers along the way, because there have been competitors for the bride's love. Unless the Lord had sovereignly and graciously drawn her and kept her close to Him, she would have been drawn away to other lovers. Her own evil heart, the world, and the devil have constantly tempted her away from her Lord's love. It is only through God's grace that this wedding feast becomes a reality.

Threat: Worldliness

In chapter 4 James focuses our attention on the threat worldliness poses for the bride of Christ. He makes clear that
love for the world is a dangerous thing, for it cannot coexist
with love for God. Friendship with one means enmity with
the other. How is the bride of Christ to escape the world's
dangers that threaten her? It is the grace of God that James
shows to be the reservoir of strength through which tried
believers can conquer the world.

The world is powerfully attractive. By nature, we are head
over heels in love with it, and even believers, after receiving
grace, continue to feel its pull. It competes for our affections
in countless and diverse ways. James understood this and
wanted the Jewish Christians to whom he was writing to be
aware of how they were being tempted by worldly desires.
Remember, many of them were poor and had endured the
loss of earthly goods. This would have been a temptation
for them, for like all of us, these Christians would have welcomed the opportunity to live by higher standards. No doubt
they missed the worldly goods they had been asked to give
up. At the beginning of chapter 4, James mentions "wars
and fightings" (v. 1) among them, which makes it clear that
things were not going well. Like all of us, they needed to be
reminded that the fulfillment of worldly desires doesn't bring
true happiness. Instead, worldly-mindedness brings conflict
and dissatisfaction to our lives.

How we need to be drawn away from the world—and
to be drawn instead to God! His grace makes such a difference. God Himself pursues us with His irresistible grace,
melting our hearts, showing us the emptiness of the world,

and making us yearn for Him. We come to see that we have been in love with the world and at enmity with God. We also learn that the world has not been an easy taskmaster. In fact, it only demands and never delivers. We're often convicted of how much time we have wasted pursuing the world and how foolish we were to set our hearts on it. But grace also shows us how much fulfillment there is to be found in God. Everything we need is in Him. There is grace to pardon us for our sins, grace to renew us after His image, grace to have an identity and purpose in this world, and grace to live a life glorifying to God. And we need this grace on a daily basis, for as long as we live; even after we've fallen out of love with the world in a fundamental, life-changing way, our hearts will be tempted to go out after the world again and again.

Can you relate to this inward struggle in the believer's heart? Do you see your need to be kept close to the heart of God, by His grace? Have you seen this especially in times of trouble? Difficulties in our lives can make us wonder whether it is worth serving the Lord. We so often feel our hearts pulled away from Him. Envy and jealousy can fill our hearts when we look at others around us who don't have to suffer in the same ways that we do. It may seem as though people who are living for the world are having a much easier time of it. We can be tempted to throw our faith overboard or at least lessen our commitment to God and get some of our satisfaction from the world. How we need to draw strength from the reservoir of God's grace at times like this! And so James points the way when he says, "He giveth more grace" (v. 6).

Misplaced Desires

Let's take a moment to think about worldliness, or conformity to the world. Worldliness exists when professing Christians give too much priority to worldly attractions, possessions, and opinions. The things we are craving may not be wrong in and of themselves. We fall into the trap of worldliness when we *set our hearts* on the things of this world, whether they are legitimate or illegitimate. At its root, worldliness is a case of *misplaced desires*. Rather than loving God above all and living for God and for His glory in this world, we are obsessed with the things of this world.

By nature, all of us live to glorify ourselves, as if this world is ours, striving for as much wealth and honor as we can get. And yet many of us don't think of ourselves as worldly, especially if we are religious people. After all, we do our religious duties. We distance ourselves from many outright evils in the world. Isn't God pleased with that? We need to live and work in the world, don't we? We can't isolate ourselves entirely from its influences. But in the meantime, we can become completely preoccupied with the here and now, setting our affections on things below and forgetting things of eternal significance.

We have already noted that the chapter opens with mention of wars and strife among these early Christians. Why were they fighting, and what were they fighting about? James writes, "Ye lust, and have not: ye kill, and desire to have, and cannot obtain: ye fight and war, yet ye have not" (v. 2). It is clear that these people wanted things they were not able to get. They were feeling unsatisfied and unfulfilled. Isn't this true of so many people in our world? The yearning for satisfaction is deeply rooted in the human heart, but it is an elusive quest. So often a feeling of emptiness characterizes the heart. It seems like the more a person tries to fill that emptiness with things, the bigger the void grows.

Sadly, many in the church are also on a frustrating quest for rest, peace, and fulfillment. In verse 3, James writes about people who "ask," but "ask amiss." He is talking about people who are praying to God for material blessings but for the wrong reason—to get ahead in the world and to enjoy more of the world. He says, "Ye ask amiss, that ye may consume it upon your lusts" (v. 3). These Christians were asking for things from God, but their motives were not pure. Enjoying the world was too much of a priority for them.

These things do not characterize a believer in his or her right place, nor do they characterize a church in its right place. The church should be marked by love for Christ, love for the brethren, self-denial, service, sobriety, and sincerity in word and deed. It is to work for the building up of the Lord's kingdom. These things are the fruit of the Spirit and the pattern for all who profess grace. They make the body of believers look different from the world and are a powerful witness to those outside the church. Only by God's grace can believers be what they need to be.

And yet often the church looks too much like the world, and believers too much like unbelievers. Why? James points to *spiritual unfaithfulness* as the root cause of the symptoms he has described. He says pointedly, "Ye adulterers and adulteresses" (4:4). In other words, worldly minded Christians are unfaithful, for they love the world and the things that are in the world (see 1 John 2:15). They have not heeded the warning that Christ gave in the Sermon on the Mount: no man can serve two masters (Matt. 6:24). James warns his readers that friendship with the world means enmity with God: "Whosoever therefore will be a friend of the world is the enemy of God" (4:4).

The "Blessing" of Frustrated Desires

We often think negatively about jealousy, and indeed, jealousy is often a sinful emotion arising from selfish motives. But jealousy can also be appropriate and right. For example, a husband or wife may jealously desire the exclusive affections of his or her spouse. In giving the law at Mount Sinai, God called Himself a "jealous God" (Ex. 20:5). This divine jealousy is pure and sinless, for He has a rightful claim on each of His creatures.

James refers to the jealousy of God in verse 5 of this chapter. There he asks, "Do ye think that the scripture saith in vain, The spirit that dwelleth in us lusteth to envy?" Commentators offer various interpretations of this verse, including one who takes it to mean that the sinful spirit that resides in human beings by nature is lustful and envious. This is certainly true, but there is a sound basis for understanding that James is referring here to the Holy Spirit, who dwells within believers (see 1 Cor. 3:16; 6:19). That Spirit is earnestly desirous to see believers living exclusively for God and is jealous when their desires are wrongly focused on things of the world rather than on God (see also Gal. 5:17). This is certainly taught in many places in Scripture (e.g., Isa. 57:16–17; 63:10).

What does it look like when the Spirit is jealous because our desires are drawn away from Him? We see a case study of this in verse 3, where James mentions those who "ask amiss" and "receive not." He is referring to people who are religious, for they are praying, but their prayers are misdirected. They are focused on worldly advancement and the like. So what does the jealous Spirit do in a case like that?

It would not do us any good if the Spirit just left us to go on desiring worldly things and getting more and more of what we desire. It is a blessing in disguise when, because a believer's desires are wrongly focused, God withholds their fulfillment. Doesn't He always give what is best? To allow His people to feed on worldly desires would be to allow them to be drawn away from Him. They would be less dependent on His grace and more distracted by worldly things. They would value the gifts over the Giver. A faithful earthly father would not give his child something dangerous, even if the child were begging for it. God, a perfect and gracious heavenly Father who always knows what is best for His children, thus overrules His people's prayers for their good.

By nature we don't see it as a blessing when God withholds the satisfaction we are looking for from material goods. Sometimes we blame God for that, perceiving Him as unkind or harsh. But frustrated desires can be sanctifying to our souls. When God shows us that we have forsaken the fountain of living waters and hewn out broken cisterns that can hold no water (Jer. 2:13), we know we need to go elsewhere to quench our thirst. Imagine that God would allow us to quench our thirst for possessions on earth. That would be a life which would end in the torment of hell, where sinners are forever thirsty and can never have their thirst quenched.

When the prodigal in the far-off country began to feel the poverty of his life (Luke 15:16–17), that was a blessing. He could no longer convince himself that he was on the right track. Instead, he was in a pigsty with corn husks he couldn't even get his hands on. What a blessed dissatisfaction he felt! For when he realized he had ruined himself, he turned back to his father and confessed his sin.

Abundant Grace

It is not enough, however, if the Lord only leaves us unsatisfied with the emptiness of the world. Remember James's promise, "He giveth more grace" (v. 6). This is the grace that brings a sinner to submit to God in humility of heart (v. 7). It is the grace of repentance that cleanses our hands and purifies our hearts (v. 8). It is the grace of mortifying the deeds of the body that we might live. It is the grace that works what Paul calls godly sorrow, which works repentance not to be repented of (2 Cor. 7:10). This is the "more grace" that God gives. It is called grace because these are changes that only God can work, despite our sin.

How does this grace work in the heart of someone whom God is drawing in love to Himself? First, *He exposes our sin.* Have you ever been listening to a sermon or reading God's Word and been convicted in your heart of how small your life was, how petty, how shameful, how sinful? Perhaps you saw something of what God had commanded you to be and how far you were from that. Perhaps God held up His good law before you, and it exposed your flaws and failings. Perhaps

He wooed you with kind invitations, and you realized how far gone you were and how hard your heart was. There are many ways in which God can show us what we really are before Him. There is so much in His Word that convicts us. In verses 7–11 of this chapter, James gives a number of commands. If we think about each of them carefully, we see how each exposes our sin. For example, James calls us to "submit [ourselves]…to God" (v. 7). We would not need this exhortation if we were not such proud sinners by nature. James says: "Resist the devil" (v. 7), which exposes our allegiance to the devil and disobedience to God. He says: "Draw nigh to God" (v. 8), which implies that we are often far from Him. Do these verses convict you of your sin? If we don't see ourselves as sinful, we will have no need to go to God and beg for His grace. We will remain in our sins.

Second, *God shows us the way back to Him*. Imagine if God left us with the knowledge of our sin but didn't show us where to turn or what to do. Ours would be only a dark despair and a fearful looking ahead for judgment (Heb. 10:27). But He does not leave us in the dark! He teaches us by His Word and Spirit what we need to do with our sin and misery. He calls us to return to Him and humble ourselves before Him (v. 10). He calls us to lay aside unholy desires and instead have God-centered desires. Our life should be characterized by a turning back to God.

Third, *God encourages us with His promises*. Notice the encouragements that James offers here. If we resist the devil, he will flee (v. 7); if we draw close to God, He will draw close to us (v. 8); if we humble ourselves in the sight of the Lord, He will lift us up (v. 10). What a gracious God! What encouragement to draw close to Him in prayer, by reading His Word, by seeking His presence, and by communing with His children. He promises that He will not stay far away but will bring His presence near. And when He does so, we will desire Him all the more. We will grow in grace. He will fulfill our heart's desire as we delight ourselves in Him (see Ps. 37:4).

Fourth, *God enables believers to do what He commands.* He is the Giver of the grace we need to obey Him, to submit to Him, and to give Him first place in our lives. He gives what John calls "grace for grace" (John 1:16). As Paul says, He "worketh in you both to will and to do of his good pleasure" (Phil. 2:13). That means that God will change our will and mind-set to seek Him and to do good to glorify Him. What need we have for this "more grace" that is promised!

Fifth, *He evokes in us a gracious spirit.* Notice how practical James becomes as he directs us in verse 11, "Speak not evil one of another, brethren." We have seen that conflicts and fighting were signs of *worldliness.* A gracious spirit toward our fellow human beings, on the other hand, is a sign of *godliness.* One who has received the grace of God becomes a channel of grace to those around him. A judgmental spirit and a readiness to speak evil of our brother are not marks of the work of God's Spirit within us.

The Reservoir of Grace

Have you seen your need to be drawn away from your love for the world and drawn toward the Lord? Have you, by grace, fallen in love with the God who made you for Himself? Or are you feeling the magnetic power of the world on your life? Do you feel like worldly desires have a hold on you?

Are you dissatisfied with your life because of the things you lack? Bring your needs to Christ, tell Him what you desire, and in this way, you can draw strength from this reservoir of God's grace. He can fulfill the needs of our lives in a way that is truly satisfying. He can even give us more than we desire—"more grace"!

God does not promise us an abundance of material goods in this life. How thankful we can be that He will not always give us everything we want! But when we live in His presence, He will shape our priorities in a way that glorifies Him. Although He doesn't give us everything we *want*, He does promise His children everything that they *need*. You can trust this faithful heavenly Father. He alone can fill our emptiness with the best fullness—with His grace!

Study Questions

1. How can trials be an opportunity for the devil to tempt us to get off the path of truth and imbibe the spirit of the world?

2. What is worldliness? Why do we often not see worldliness for what it is?

3. Why does it seem so difficult for the church, or for churches, to get along? Think about a past or present situation in your church. According to this chapter, what is a root cause of quarreling between people? What would happen if verses 11 and 12 were taken seriously in our churches? How can this happen?

4. Name specific ways in which we can draw nearer to God. What does James tell us will be the result?

5. What do you think will change when we live near to God? Will this be visible to those around you? How?

6. Do you discern differences in your desires when you draw closer to God? In what way? Be as specific as you can.

7. What does God's jealousy mean for our lives? Practically speaking, how do we live exclusively for Him? What desires and passions in your own life stand in the way of this?

THE WILL OF GOD

James 4:13–17

Trials have a way of making us feel the fundamental instability of life on earth. When things are going well, we might take the next ten, twenty, or fifty years for granted. But when something happens that shakes us up—when we receive an alarming medical diagnosis, when a family member gets in an accident or becomes seriously sick, or when we face a sudden change in financial or social status—our view of the future may take a dramatic turn for the worse. We might even become depressed or despairing, unable to believe that things will ever change for the better. We might sense a loss of control that is hard to endure. Our dreams and plans for the future look as though they may no longer become reality.

How true it is that the future may not go as we have planned. That is the reality of life. James knows, however, that it is not necessarily bad for us to become more realistic about the future. In fact, if trials cause us to see life from the perspective of the perfect will of God, we can be happier as a result. When blessed by God, trials can make us more confident rather than less confident. This is because our confidence becomes more grounded in God and in His perfect will than in the changing circumstances of life.

Our Strong Self-Will

Sometimes parents will describe their child as having a strong will. A strong-willed child is determined and headstrong and may find submitting to others challenging. Other children are seen as more flexible, less headstrong, and easier going. But in a certain sense, we are all strong-willed by nature. Our own wants and desires are of primary importance to us. We may be more or less easygoing in our outward demeanor, but none of us likes having our wills crossed. We want what we want—it is as simple as that!

Certainly, when planning for the future, we all tend to focus too much on our own plans without regarding God's plan for our lives and our time. Our attitude toward the future can often be boiled down to two words: I will. James warns against this attitude when he writes: "Go to now, ye that say, To day or to morrow we will go...continue...buy... sell...get gain" (v. 13). James wants us to see the foolishness of speaking with certainty about what we are going to do. We act so confident about our plans, but the future is not ours to claim.

We may think we will do something, but often, if we get started at all, we only end up making a beginning of our plans. We may change our minds, or lose interest in what we first planned, or decide to do something else instead. God alone is eternal and unchanging. He alone is without beginning and without end. And He alone is able to execute everything that He wills. He does it perfectly, all the time.

Meanwhile, we talk as if what we wish for and plan will become reality. Think about the rich fool in the parable that Christ told: "I will pull down my barns, and build greater" (Luke 12:18). Similarly, Isaiah portrays the Babylonian king saying in his heart, "I will ascend into heaven" (Isa. 14:13). Pharaoh said, "I will pursue, I will overtake" (Ex. 15:9). But in each case, plans were foiled. God effectively answered each of these men, "You will not."

Verse 13 gives us a close look at this confident self-determination that so often motivates us. Notice all the assumptions that the person speaking here makes, and ask yourself how often you have made similar ones:

- There will be a tomorrow.
- I will be alive and healthy today and tomorrow.
- I will be able to travel safely to a city, where I will do business.
- I will be safe and healthy throughout the coming year.
- I will acquire and sell goods.
- My business transactions will bring me gain.

Do you see all the leaps this man is taking in his thinking? He is counting on so much! And how much our own thinking mirrors this man's. How many of our calendars are summed up by the attitude portrayed in James 4:13? How many investment portfolios reflect the mentality of the man in this verse? How many business forecasts could be taken straight out of verse 13? This is the mentality that keeps our societies buzzing with excitement and energy. Success gurus tell us to think positively and envision ourselves accomplishing all the things we would like to do. How important it is not to allow ourselves to presume upon the future.

Our Real Ignorance

James responds to this presumptive attitude with these humbling words: "Ye know not" (v. 14). We say, "Today or tomorrow I will." James reminds us that we can't even be sure that we will see tomorrow, much less how tomorrow will look.

How often have we gone into a day filled with "I wills" and been stopped with the reality that "I don't know." Some unexpected event, some surprising twist in providence, a sudden phone call, and our ignorance of the future is exposed. We say to each other, "I never expected this to happen," or, "I never would have thought today would have turned out like this."

"You don't know," James says. It is a sobering thing to face up to how little we know about the future. Knowing God is the only source of such confidence.

It is a blessing if the trials that God sends into our lives help us realize our limitations. After all, we are only mortal creatures; while God is eternal, we are transient. The Bible often reminds us of the brevity of life. Life is compared to a shadow (Ps. 144:4; Eccl. 6:12), a wind (Ps. 78:39), and a handbreadth (Ps. 39:5). Ecclesiastes 1 reminds us of the vanity of life. Psalm 39:5 tells us, "Every man at his best state is altogether vanity." And Psalm 144:4 points out, "Man is like to vanity." The Hebrew word translated as "vanity" literally means "vapor." That is all life is. Vapor is something that you can't clutch in your hands or hang on to. What reminders these are to see life differently from how we are so prone to see it! Nineteenth-century preacher Charles Spurgeon wrote: "We cannot reckon upon the clouds, their laws are so variable, and their conditions so obscure. Such also is our life…. Why do we choose to build upon clouds, and pile our palaces on vapour, to see them melt away, as aforetime they have often melted?"[1]

It is best to learn early about how unsure the future is and how powerless we are to bring about what we will. We ought to go to the One who can teach us what we need to know about planning for the future. We can rely on His knowledge of the future!

True Freedom

It is truly freeing when we learn to turn away from our own will and ask that God's will be done in our lives. After all, because God is only good, His will is also only good. It takes grace for us, fallen sinners that we are, to acknowledge that, but God can bring us there. He brought strong-willed Saul of Tarsus to the point where he asked, "What wilt thou have me to do?" (Acts 9:6).

Learning to look for and follow God's will brings happiness and contentment. After all, only God can speak an unchanging "I will." The Lord says in Isaiah, "Yea, I have spoken it, I will also bring it to pass; I have purposed it, I will also do it" (46:11). Scripture assures us that the Lord does all that He purposes to do. Let's not act as if we can be like God.

---

1. C. H. Spurgeon, "God's Will about the Future," in *The Metropolitan Tabernacle Pulpit* (Pasadena, Tex.: Pilgrim Publications), 38:61–72. This sermon was published the week that Spurgeon died (January 31, 1892).

Let's not imagine that we can accomplish everything that we plan; instead, let's trust in the God whose good will cannot be thwarted.

If we have no real knowledge of what the future might bring, does this mean that there is no use at all in planning for it? Is there no place for weekly planners or retirement accounts? A cynical person might feel that way. But neither does Scripture suggest an attitude of negligence about the future. Prudent planning for what lies ahead is wise and necessary (see Prov. 6:6–8; 21:5; 24:27; Luke 14:28). What James is doing here is putting our planning for the future into its proper perspective and showing us what the Christian's heart attitude should be: "For that ye ought to say, If the Lord will, we shall live, and do this, or that" (v. 15).

It is still common in some Christian circles to use the acronym "D.V." behind dates of planned activities. This stands for the Latin *Deo volente* (the Lord willing). When used meaningfully, it expresses the thought that our plans are contingent upon the permission and blessing of the Lord. We shouldn't use the expression flippantly, though. In the same sermon quoted above, Spurgeon wrote: "You know, it is a fine thing when you can put your religion into Latin, and make it very short. Then nobody knows what you mean by it; or, if they do, they can praise your scholarship, and admire your humility." His point is well taken. We do not fulfill the intent of James 4:15 simply by using the letters "D.V." behind the dates we are planning. What we need is a heart attitude of reliance and waiting upon the Lord and His will for the future.

Our Happy Dependence

How can we obey James's call for a heartfelt dependence on God for the future? Let me suggest five things that go into living dependently on God's will. If, with God's help, we do these things, we will find freedom and joy in submission to His plan for our lives.

1. *We should not put too much stock in our own will.* We have all kinds of ideas about how things in our life should go. As we saw, our wills are strong, but we are also fickle. Have you ever wanted something badly, but then, after you had it awhile, you wondered why you ever wanted it at all? Also, remember how powerless our wills are. We cannot perform the least thing, if God's providence forbids it. So we should learn happily to resign our will to the perfect will of God, even when it is different from what we may have expected or wanted.

2. *We should admire God's will.* God's wisdom is magnificent and so infinitely above ours. He has willed all things from before time began. His will is greater than our life. He can will billions of things at the same time, none of which are wrong or imperfect. Moreover, He brought our life into being and will sustain it until its appointed end, not a moment too soon or too late. Let's be thankful that His will, not ours, governs things.

3. *We should obey God's revealed will.* When James says, "If the Lord will," he is speaking of God's

providential will. But if our life depends on His providential will, it must conform to His revealed will, as we find it in Scripture. Obedience to His Word is nonnegotiable. It is in God's Son that we see God's will most clearly revealed. Christ said it most perfectly: "I seek not mine own will, but the will of the Father which hath sent me" (John 5:30).

4. *We should lean on God's promises.* Many of the promises of the Bible are phrased with the Lord's "I wills." "I will put enmity between thee and the woman" (Gen. 3:15). "I will love them freely.... I will be as the dew unto Israel" (Hos. 14:4–5). "I will restore health unto thee, and I will heal thee of thy wounds" (Jer. 30:17). "I will never leave thee, nor forsake thee" (Heb. 13:5). We should plead these promises and make them our hope, for they are solid and lasting and bring ultimate good into our lives.

5. *We must cherish each moment of life as a gift of God.* James says, "If the Lord will, we shall live" (v. 15). In other words, God's will governs our life. God is behind every breath we breathe and every move we make. Life is not summed up by the plans we make, the actions we perform, or the things we achieve. It is God's plan unfolding. Let's stop and consider life as an immense gift of God. This will help us live it dependently.

The Reservoir of God's Will

Perhaps you are in the difficult process of learning that the great plans you made for yourself are not going to work out. This is not easy, especially when you are asked to experience sickness, loss, and grief. It is hard to be faced with the reality that we can't control our future or follow through on our plans. We may feel especially confused if we thought our plans were in line with God's will.

Many of the Lord's people have discovered that God's will for them was different from what they saw as best initially. Such a discovery may be a long and painful process, but it offers opportunity for learning important lessons. We don't see as God sees. We don't know as God knows. We may never learn in this life why God's will had to be so different from our own. But freedom and joy do come when we learn to submit to God's will. We may rest in the knowledge that God does what is best for us and that He takes care of our needs.

God's perfect will for us is a great reservoir from which we can draw strength when we feel weak and discouraged. He has said that He has plans to give His people a future and an expected end (Jer. 29:11). Wouldn't it be terrible to have to live with the idea that God's power is not enough to accomplish His will? Could you live with a god who might will something but is quite powerless to achieve it? No, it is far better to submit to the will of a good and good-doing God. Remember, He is the God and Father of Jesus Christ. His will is made known perfectly to us in the gift of His Son. Because of Christ, we can have a future in fellowship with God, walking according to His perfect will. If we follow Him with a submissive heart, He will not lead us astray.

Study Questions

1. In Matthew 6:25–34, part of the Sermon on the Mount, Jesus speaks about how we should view the future. How are James's thoughts similar to the Lord's teaching?

2. Summarize, in one sentence, what the Christian's attitude toward the future should be.

3. What are the benefits of submitting to God's will? Can you think of any promises in Scripture connected to this?

4. Have you ever been afraid to let go of control of your life? What areas or plans in your life are you holding on to most?

5. How can we actively submit to God's will, and how does this become practical in your life?

6. What does verse 17 teach us? Give some examples of what James means here.

THE JUSTICE OF GOD

James 5:1–11

When we compare the lives of the wicked with the lives of the righteous on this side of eternity, it may seem like the wicked are better off. Those who live ungodly and selfish lives often have riches and pleasure, while those who serve God are often poor and afflicted. But as we saw when we studied the truth of God, things are not always what they seem. If we look at life in the light of God's righteousness and the final judgment, which He says will most certainly set things right, we need not be deceived by appearances.

The psalm writer Asaph struggled because injustice seemed to reign in his world. He observed "the prosperity of the wicked" (Ps. 73:3). They were strong, untroubled, proud, violent, fat, corrupt, and rebellious in their speech (see verses 4–9 of that psalm), yet their success seemed unshakeable. This was hard for Asaph to understand. He lamented, "When I thought to know this, it was too painful for me; until I went into the sanctuary of God; then understood I their end" (Ps. 73:16–17). Somehow, in the temple, Asaph came to see the truth of God's justice, which would most surely set everything right in the end (see Ps. 73:18–20). He realized he had been foolish not to think of that before.

What a warning this is to remember that a day of reckoning is coming. Just because people seem to get away with murder, injustice, and oppression all around us doesn't mean that the Judge of the earth won't do right, as Abraham said long ago (Gen. 18:25). Judgment could come at any time! It is not surprising that, in light of this, James calls those who have lived materialistic lives to "weep and howl" (v. 1), because the things they are trusting in for security and satisfaction are rusting and corroding before their very eyes.

On the other hand, God's children, even if they are oppressed, should persevere patiently (vv. 7–8). Like Asaph, they may be comforted by the truth of God's justice. Human judges sometimes fail in their application of justice, and criminals often walk free. But we have no reason to fear that God's justice will fail. What may seem unjust now will appear gloriously just on the great day of reckoning—and that day is not far off. As James says, the coming of the Lord draws near (v. 8), and the Judge stands at the door (v. 9). Doesn't this perspective help put things in their proper light? This can help give us the focus we need in a world where things often seem upside down.

The Vanity of a Materialistic Life

James begins chapter 5 taunting those who have invested themselves only in this world and not in Christ. He calls them to mourn because the things they are living for, their riches and possessions, are slipping through their fingers (vv. 1–6). He pinpoints what their actions have deserved and when they will be given their just rewards. In a word, he faces them with the day of reckoning. Let's look at three things brought out about the ungodly.

First, *James points out to them that their "heaven" is crumbling before their eyes* (vv. 1–3). He is harking back to something Christ said when He was on earth—namely, that earthly treasures will not last (Matt. 6:19–20). The rich have no shield against rust and moths. Precious things don't last; they soon decay. The millionaire is powerless against the forces of corrosion and oxidation. His rusting Rolls-Royce or his moth-eaten golf shirts cry out to him, "Your self-made paradise is coming to an end!"

When we look around us in this world, don't we see the truth of what James is saying? The lifestyle of materialism and consumerism that beckons us today will only leave us empty and unfulfilled. It cannot keep its promises of lasting happiness and satisfaction. Even if it might satisfy us temporarily, such happiness will not last. We need only to open our trash bins, forage through our basements, or look through our grandmother's jewelry boxes to see the handwriting on the wall.

Second, *James makes clear that fraudulent practices cry out for retribution* (vv. 4, 6). In every age, people have been tempted to increase their own wealth by dealing fraudulently with others. There are many forms of injustice against others. Withholding wages from employees, robbing from employers, and not paying taxes owed to the government are just a few examples. The human heart is by nature covetous, wanting to have more than it deserves. But there is One who sees and knows all things. The Judge of all the earth will do right. He keeps a divine record of everything, including unpaid wages and owed taxes. Changes in the numbers on the accounting ledger do not escape His eye. Every sin is recorded in the divine books, and He will mete out judgment perfectly.

As Christians, our lives should be characterized by justice, equity, and generosity. This includes giving others the honor, respect, and trust they deserve. It also includes stewarding the wealth we have received from God. It means not hoarding what He has given to us but sharing it with others and using it for the building up of God's kingdom. Everything we have has been given to us by God not to consume on ourselves but to enjoy with thankful hearts and to share with those who are worse off than we are. There is great happiness and a great witness in giving back to God and to others from what we have been given.

Third, *James declares that the pleasure the wicked enjoy on earth is simply the equivalent of being fattened for the slaughterhouse* (v. 5). That is certainly not a fate to be envied. We don't envy animals being fed well every day in preparation for butchering. So the sumptuous living of many is no proof that they will enjoy God's favor in eternity. The opposite is often the case.

The Full Harvest God's Children Will Enjoy

In verse 7 James shifts his focus as he addresses the "brethren." He teaches them what the godly should do when the wicked prosper. Should they adopt the ways of the wicked in order to gain wealth as well? Should they be envious and complain? Should they take up the sword and demand justice for themselves? Should they break out in cursing or make rash oaths? These are all things that James's readers may have been tempted to do. But James teaches them to deal with injustice in a different way (vv. 7–11). This was not a time for rashness or unrestrained emotions. The great need of the hour was for patience.

James mentions patience four times in five verses. In the context of this study, we could define "patience" as the virtue, found in a heart graced by God, which looks to God and waits for Him to act. It perseveres in waiting on God, no matter how long it takes for God to fulfill His word or promise.

James helps his readers understand what patience is by using the analogy of a harvest. A farmer needs to patiently wait for the harvest. If he began harvesting the moment he saw some fruit forming, he would lose everything. There is no hurrying the ripening of his crops. Notice that James mentions the early and latter rains (v. 7). In Israel, rains fall heavily during October and November and again during March and April. The early rains loosen the ground, which is helpful during the fall planting season. The spring rains help ripen the harvest. Just as a farmer needs to be patient and let his crops ripen fully, so believers must exercise patience till the great Husbandman returns for His full harvest.

James unpacks the duty of patience in four parts. First, *James emphasizes the need for stability of heart.* He writes: "Be ye also patient; stablish your hearts" (v. 8). The connection James makes between patience and stability is helpful; these two virtues support each other. Patient looking to the Lord will steady our otherwise unstable hearts, which are so often pulled back and forth by all kinds of emotions and reactions to circumstances. Psalm 27:14 promises that when we wait on the Lord and are of good courage, He will strengthen our heart. Stabilizing ourselves on Christ, our rock, helps us exercise patience in waiting for the Lord to answer our prayers. Everything else other than Christ is sinking sand.

Second, *James teaches us to look not to others, but to God, who will come* (v. 9). So often our gaze is only horizontal, and we focus on the people around us. We spend our time comparing ourselves to them, thinking about what they have that we don't and seeing injustices that need to be made right. Instead, our gaze should center on the Lord. He is coming again as the perfect Judge. At His return, everything wrong will be set right. Every injustice that was done on the earth will be set right by the Judge who knows and sees everything and judges perfectly. What a day that will be!

Third, *James suggests as models the suffering saints of Scripture* (vv. 10–11). We should take encouragement from the examples of believers from former times. James specifically mentions the prophets. Think of Jeremiah, who suffered so much as his people were being taken away captive. He was even thrown into a pit and left to die. Or think of Daniel, who was thrown into the lions' den. These men put their trust in God, even in dark circumstances. They endured and persevered in affliction. James also mentions Job. Job was especially tried and tested by God. Although at times he spoke unwisely, in the end he staked his hopes on the Lord and on His mercy and compassion. We should emulate this attitude of patience in suffering. Look to God's character and cherish His promises. He is the faithful God, and His word is sure and steadfast. He truly is the God who pities and who is full of tender mercy (v. 11).

Fourth, *James again points to our speech as an area where we should be especially cautious* (v. 12). This time he mentions swearing and taking oaths. Rather than relying on them as a standard of truth-telling, our word should always be reliable. When we say yes, we should mean yes, and when we say no, we should mean no. James's teaching here echoes the teaching of the Lord Jesus in His Sermon on the Mount (see Matt. 5:33–37). Neither of these passages forbids taking oaths and swearing when we are asked to do so for a legitimate and lawful reason, but both emphasize the need for honesty. Our speech should be trustworthy at all times, not only when we are under oath.

You may be wondering what this has to do with the subject of patience. Isn't it true that when we are suffering, we sometimes speak too quickly or rashly? We may complain or murmur, throw blame around, and even make rash oaths that we don't intend to keep. When we are impatient with how providence is directing our lives, the temptation to speak foolishly can be very strong. Speaking rashly may lead to mistakes we will regret. So as we seek God's help to cultivate a patient spirit, we should especially guard our tongues (see Ps. 39:1). As he wrote this, perhaps James was thinking of Job, who made heated statements that he later regretted. At any rate, James is emphasizing how quickly we can sin with our tongues. Let's pray for grace to be, as James wrote earlier, swift to hear and slow to speak (1:19).

What to Do While We Wait

Perhaps as you are reading this you are remembering how you have been hurt or injured in the past by someone who professed to be a Christian. Or perhaps you are a victim of oppression or injustice right now. What can be done? Though patience is important, James is not teaching us that we may only sit back passively and wait for God's justice to make things right. Appropriate action can be taken. We may seek to have injustice redressed for ourselves or for others. We are given clear directions for addressing wrongs in Matthew 18:15–20.

Also, in both personal life and church life, we should follow the example of Christ, who stood up for those who were unjustly treated and oppressed. Rather than falling into the materialistic mind-set of our culture and turning a blind eye to the poor and oppressed, we should take a special interest in them. James has already emphasized this in 1:27, when he told his readers to visit widows and orphans in their affliction. There are people around us who need our care. Do we actively pursue opportunities to minister to those less fortunate than ourselves, offering a helping hand and a cup of cold water?

The Reservoir of God's Justice

Psalm 37 helps put everything in perspective. It reminds us that God still rules even when things around us seem to be topsy-turvy, and He will judge in righteousness in the end. We should be thankful that it is not our place to mete out justice, for we could never do it rightly. And having to wait for God's justice can be a blessing if it cultivates patience and submission and helps us leave things in God's hands, as Psalm 37 instructs us to do (vv. 4–9).

Surprising strength will flow to us as we commit our cause to Him and in patience possess our souls (Luke 21:19).

We will pray for our enemies and even seek their conversion, realizing that if God left us to ourselves, we would meet His just judgment, and what a terrible end would be ours. The cross of Christ is the best place to be as we reflect on the truth that He satisfied the justice of God for all His people, in order that they would not be condemned as they deserve.

So let's lay aside all thoughts of jealousy or revenge and instead love those who wrong us. Let's pray that God would work in them before His judgment comes, and it is too late. And let's pray for patient hearts, which wait like a farmer anticipating a full harvest. You will not be disappointed if you wait for Him.

Study Questions

1. What does it mean to lay up (or store) treasures in heaven, as Matthew 6:20 teaches us to do? Name some of these treasures.

2. Describe the "harvest" that James speaks of in verse 7.

3. Why is grudging (which we could think of as complaining) not compatible with patience (v. 9)? How can we mortify the tendency to complain?

4. While encouraging patience, James calls the Lord both "the judge" (v. 9) and "very pitiful," or compassionate (v. 11). Some might think these are contradictory descriptions. But how can they both be encouraging to the believer?

5. What promises does God give to believers for their life here? Are you actively or passively waiting for those to be fulfilled? How can you adopt a positive, active attitude toward God's promises?

6. What role does prayer have in your life? How can this bring God's promises closer?

THE EAR OF GOD

James 5:12–20

Some people think these final verses of the book of James are simply a string of unrelated thoughts touching on various points of church life. Anointing sick members of the church, confessing faults to each other, praying like Elijah, and turning people back from their errors are all addressed. But these aren't just assorted bits of instruction; that is not how James has been writing up to this point, and that is not how he concludes. The common thread running through these verses is the subject of prayer.

When we pray during times of trial, we put our weakness into God's strong hands and give our insufficiency over to His sufficiency. We tap into God's great resources of compassion and love. So these verses are pointing us to the God who hears and answers prayer. Isn't this an appropriate way for James to conclude his letter? What better spiritual and pastoral guidance could he give than to point his readers to the God who encourages, hears, and answers prayer?

Praying in Famine

An important clue to how this section holds together can be found in James's mention of Elijah in the middle of it (vv. 17–18). In some ways, circumstances in Elijah's day were not very different from those of James's day. In Elijah's day, the rich oppressed the poor, living in luxury without any regard for the Lord. The people of Israel had compromised with the world and committed spiritual unfaithfulness under the leadership of Ahab and Jezebel. As a result, God sent calamities upon His people, and He sent His thundering prophet Elijah. Elijah, as it were, put the nation under spiritual discipline. He called on God to close the heavens so that it would not rain. As a result, there was a famine, which God had threatened if the people were to forsake Him (Deut. 11:17).

But that was not the end of the story. When three and a half years had passed, Elijah called the people together on Mount Carmel and confronted them with their sin—they had halted between two opinions. But there on the mountain, he also prayed fervently for them: "Hear me, O LORD, hear me, that this people may know that thou art the LORD God, and that thou hast turned their heart back again" (1 Kings 18:37).

Elijah was a man who lived close to the Lord. He was poor, materially speaking, but very rich, spiritually speaking. God had taught him to pray. As Elijah leaned on the strong arms of God in prayer for the nation, God showed His power in answer to Elijah's prayers. Marvelously, the discipline was removed. The heavens opened again, and rain came down to water the earth. Elijah was a prophet who spoke God's word when God's people were in the midst of much compromise.

Through difficult providences God was pursuing His way-ward people. God blessed Elijah's ministry, and through the instrumentality of Elijah's prayers, He turned the nation back from their idolatry and evil ways.

In his early New Testament days, James carries Elijah's mission forward. He challenges the people to turn back to God *in truth*, not just superficially. He stands ready to pray and encourages others to pray. He gives comfort to those who mourn and shows the way the sick will be healed. Like Elijah was, James shows himself a true servant of God in his genera-tion. The ending verses of this epistle are a fitting description of both Elijah and James: "Brethren, if any of you do err from the truth, and one convert him; let him know, that he which converteth the sinner from the error of his way shall save a soul from death, and shall hide a multitude of sins" (vv. 19–20).

Praying in Affliction

It may not be natural to think like this, but it is helpful to see difficulties in life as invitations to pray. This is essentially what James says in verse 13: "Is any among you afflicted? let him pray." How important prayer is and how much there is to pray about, both for ourselves and for others! The world is full of needs in our families, churches, neighborhoods, cit-ies, and nations. You don't have to go far before you can find someone desperately in need of prayer. And the more press-ing the need, the more pressing the invitation to prayer.

Think about it: What better thing can we do with our needs than pray about them? We may be tempted to do many other things with our problems—dwell on them, blame other people for them, fret about them, try to escape them, or look to the people around us for help with them. But rather than suggesting any of these things, James says, "Pray." Let the person who is sick find a place where he can bow his knees and pour out his soul to God, bringing his need before the almighty One. True prayer, one of the chief parts of true religion, takes shelter in God and finds solutions in His infinite wisdom.

Another important element of true religion, as well as a fitting response to answered prayer, is praise. James goes on to counsel, "Is any merry? let him sing psalms" (v. 13). James's reference to the book of Psalms is a helpful one, for this great book of Scripture models both prayer and praise for us. We find both the low pitch of prayer and the high pitch of song there. Every true believer knows these two attitudes of heart. In a way, they can be said to encapsulate all of true religion. On the one hand, a believer cries out in times of need. And on the other hand, when God brings him out of all his distresses, he sings for joy because of the bountiful blessings God has bestowed upon him.

Cares into Prayers

This is James's first emphasis in these verses about prayer: *we should turn our cares into prayers and our thanksgivings into praises.* Prayer and praise are both ways of communing with God, no matter what our situation is. They are a reflecting back to God about our circumstances. Remember that chapter 4 encourages us to draw near to God with the promise that when we do so, He will draw near to us. Involving God in the circumstances of our lives through prayer is a means to that closeness and fellowship. As we would communicate with a good friend about even the small details of life, we should seek the presence of the Friend who sticks closer than a brother (Prov. 18:24) through both prayer and praise.

Second, *we should seek the prayers of God's people, especially those in church office* (v. 14a). Sometimes Christians are reluctant to tell others in their church family about their needs. Some people like their privacy and are afraid that people will pry into their lives. Others are scared that their news will be spread around and gossiped about. But things should be different in a church community. When we have a need, as it is appropriate, we should not be ashamed to tell fellow believers and the leaders of the church about it. This verse also implies a duty of leaders in the church: they are to take a warm interest in those who are sick in their congregation. Caring for the body of Christ includes caring for physical needs. The prayers of God's servants from the pulpit, in private, at a prayer meeting, or at the bedside are all part of what James is speaking of in verse 14.

Third, *we should combine prayer with using means to address our needs* (v. 14b). When James mentions oil, he does not mean to refer to extreme unction, as in the Roman Catholic Church, or some superstitious ritual, such as those used in the different faith-healing movements today. Rather, the Bible often describes oil as having a medicinal purpose (Isa. 1:6; Mark 6:13; Luke 10:34). Basically, James is saying, use prayer *and* available medicines or means of recovery. In His goodness, God has given us many things in nature and through science that can help alleviate pain or even cure diseases. We should not despise these things, but use them in an attitude of dependence on the Lord rather than on ourselves or modern medicine.

Fourth, *we should pray believingly* (v. 15). James has already warned against wavering in prayer and being double-minded (1:6–8). If we pray simply as a means to an end that we have already determined beforehand, we cannot expect God to honor our prayers. Believing prayer is submissive yet confident prayer. It trusts in God that His will is always good. Like the faith of Job, who is mentioned in verse 11, this faith trusts God, even if He should slay us (Job 13:15). Mind you, this verse is not a "name it and claim it" promise. God has not promised to heal every sickness on this side of eternity. In 2 Timothy 4:20 Paul mentions a man named Trophimus, whom he left sick at Miletum; the implication in this verse is that Paul was not able to heal Trophimus of whatever was ailing him. Prayers for physical healing are not always answered. Death is part of the curse, and often sickness is the chariot ordained by God to carry His people through death into His presence. But if we could count how many Christians have been prayed for at one time or other and been healed, either in an ordinary or extraordinary way, we would see the faithfulness of God in honoring this word. And note well, there is a promise that will come true, whether or not physical healing is granted: we will draw closer to God's presence, and God will draw closer to us.

Fifth, *we should pray fervently* (vv. 16–18). James prods us to fervent prayer by reminding us of Elijah. As we have seen, through Elijah's prayers the heavens were closed, and it did not rain for years. But when he bowed with his face to the ground on Mount Carmel and prayed for rain, the skies again poured down rain on the parched ground. We might be prone to say, "But I can never be like Elijah. I could never presume to be such a holy man." But, James says, Elijah was like us! He was a man "subject to like passions as we are" (v. 17). He too felt discouraged, fearful, alone, rejected, and despondent. Yet God heard his fervent prayers. What encouragement for us to keep praying, regardless of where we find ourselves! Should we not storm the mercy seat of God and knock on His door until He opens?

Does Praying Work?

But, you may be wondering, does prayer really work? Sometimes when people tell us they are praying for us or when they ask us to pray about something, we might secretly wonder, is it going to change things? Does prayer really help? The answer is that prayer does change things, but not always in the way we are looking for or expecting. Remember, prayer is a means to closeness and fellowship with God. And as we commune with Him, *we* change, even if nothing else does. So whether our situation changes or not is secondary, for we change and become different in our situation, and perhaps that is what God wants.

And many times the Lord does answer our prayers directly. If we honestly look back over the years, hasn't it been true that "the prayer of faith shall save the sick, and the Lord shall raise him up" (v. 15)? How many times have people who have been prayed for by others been healed? Haven't so many of our temporal needs been provided for in answer to our prayers? And let's not forget to look beyond the tangible in seeking answers to prayer. Isn't His work of grace in the

heart the most important thing we can pray for, for ourselves
and for others? If you are a believer, it is likely that you were
prayed for by others who saw your spiritual need and brought
it to the Lord, asking Him for His work in your heart. Be
encouraged to pray for the souls of others. God also answers
those prayers, as the second part of verse 15 says: "and if
he have committed sins, they shall be forgiven him." Let us
never minimize the value of prayer both for spiritual needs
and for temporal ones.

The Strong Hands of the Shepherd

James has been giving pastoral guidance throughout this
epistle. He has been a shepherd of souls, directing people
who have lost their strength back to God, His unchangeable
truth, His family, His friendship, His wisdom, His will, and
His justice. Now, as he ends his epistle, he points them to
experiencing God's presence through prayer.

Aren't all these things to which James has been pointing
reservoirs to draw strength from when all strength is gone?
Trials drain our strength, but God can renew our strength.
As a Shepherd, He does lead us to green pastures and to still
waters—reservoirs that strengthen us.

So, with the tenderness of a shepherd, James seeks to
draw souls back to the Great Shepherd in this epistle. How
fitting that he ends with a beautiful picture of how a believer
can also be a shepherd of souls: "Brethren, if any of you do
err from the truth, and one convert him; let him know, that
he which converteth the sinner from the error of his way
shall save a soul from death, and shall hide a multitude of
sins" (vv. 19–20). Believers are to care for the spiritual needs

around them, for they are used by God to draw souls to Him. Both believers and unbelievers need spiritual care, for both, like sheep, are prone to wander and stray from God's truth. Believers show something of their Lord's character as they seek to draw those around them to the Lord, for the first time or again.

Still Waters

Micah 7:7 says: "My God will hear me." What a comfort that, as God's children cry, the Lord hears them. He is the Good Shepherd who knows His sheep. Even their silent sighs, deep groans, and barely audible whimpers are known by Him. He has planted them in their hearts by His Spirit (Rom. 8:26).

As sinners, we don't deserve that God should hear our prayers. But He is a gracious and merciful God who does hear. He hears the needy when they cry, and He answers in the way that best fulfills His purposes and glorifies His name. None of His sheep will perish. He will pardon their sins and save their souls from death. Through Christ's finished work, the salvation of all His people is secure in God. He will not forsake the work that His strong hands have begun.

The Good Shepherd will go ahead of His flock, leading them again and again to reservoirs of strength. All the reservoirs of God are full of strength—His truth, His lordship, His friendship, His wisdom, His grace, His will, His justice, and His ear. Sometimes we need one of these reservoirs and at other times another—but God leads His people to the fullness that is in Him. He knows us all by name and will lead us, through trials and dark valleys, to green pastures. Pray that God will guide you too, that you will not walk astray but follow Him closely every day of your life. Then the promises that He gives will accompany you on the way and will give you all you need. You will lack nothing.

Study Questions

1. What things can stand in the way of fervent prayer? Do we sometimes give up too easily? How can we learn to pray fervently?

2. Describe a time when you felt that God answered your prayer as you "kept knocking."

3. Why is it that we need reminders to praise God during times of joy? What does this show us about what our attitude toward God and His blessings often is?

4. What are some practical ways you can help fulfill the church's responsibility toward the sick?

5. So often we think ourselves unable to attain what Bible characters attained. How does verse 17 turn that impression on its head? Do you see your own character described in Elijah's? How?

6. Have you ever gone through a time of trial during which you prayed often but did not see your outward circumstances changing? Did you notice changes in yourself and your own thinking as you drew near to God in prayer? Describe that time.

7. In what practical ways can we reach out to those who are erring from the truth (see v. 20)? What potential outcome should motivate us to do that?